Willy Brandt · Peace

Willy Brandt

PEACE

Writings and Speeches
of the
Nobel Peace Prize Winner
1971

Verlag
Neue Gesellschaft GmbH

Published by the Friedrich-Ebert-Stiftung
Edited by Klaus Reiff

1971 by the Publishing House:
Verlag Neue Gesellschaft GmbH,
53 Bonn-Bad Godesberg, Kölner Straße 149
Germany

The Nobel Foundation kindly gave the permission to publish
Willy Brandt's speech "Peach Policy in Our Time"

Picture: Bundesbildstelle, Sven Simon, AP, dpa, Landesbildstelle Berlin
Cover: Uwe Loesch, 4 Düsseldorf
Produced by Union-Druckerei und Verlagsanstalt GmbH, 6 Frankfurt/Main
Printed in Germany 1971

Federal President Gustav W. Heinemann

Nobel Peace Prize for Willy Brandt

In the world of today endangered in so many ways, the peoples are looking for men and women who deserve confidence. The award of the Nobel Peace Prize to Federal Chancellor Willy Brandt by the Committee appointed by the Norwegian Parliament has in the unanimity of its decision made clear that in him it sees a man worthy of such confidence. In it, there is at the same time agreeable recognition of the striving of our people for reconciliation and good neighbourly relations with the peoples in West and East, in North and South.

For many decades, the neighbouring peoples have regarded us as a disturber of the peace. Particularly after the last war, which brought such infinite misery to large parts of the world, we were surrounded by profound mistrust and even hate.

Through the award of the Nobel Peace Prize to Chancellor Willy Brandt is expressed the fact that another Germany lives for the world's feelings today, — a Germany, from which emanates a great endeavour to achieve détente and to uphold peace among the peoples.

Those awarding the Nobel Peace Prize see in Willy Brandt, in the story of his personal life and in his political actions a German politician who combines fairness and tolerance, but who is also firmly determined in defiance of much resistance to pave the way into a peaceful future for his people. The worldwide response which came through to us after the award of the Nobel Peace Prize is an indication of what is expected of us.

Confidence is binding. We shall have to make sure that we justify it. This means that fairness and tolerance inwardly and outwardly must remain the basis, from which German policy derives its strength.

We are called on to promote everything which we, together with our neighbours, can do for peace in the world. Only a constant striving of this kind can give our people that inward and outward security which is necessary in order to bring our national problems as well closer to solution. The peoples yearn for peace in the world. Our people — and I am sure of this — will not after all that has happened slacken in its striving to include us in worldwide detente with the goal of upholding peace.

When Federal Chancellor Willy Brandt receives the Nobel Peace Prize in Oslo on Dezember 10th, he will be doing so on behalf of all people who want to live in peace in their way.

Federal President Gustav W. Heinemann

Nobel Peace Prize for Willy Brandt

Reasons Given by the Nobel Committee

During the whole of the postwar period, the politically unsolved German question has constituted a latent danger to the peace. During these years, many attempts have been made to assert détente within this danger sphere of political tension.

The Nobel Committee of the Norwegian Parliament has today awarded the Peace Prize to Federal Chancellor Willy Brandt. With this choice, the Committee has attempted to implement the intentions of the will of Alfred Nobel. As leader of the Federal Republic of Germany and in the name of the German people, Willy Brandt has stretched out his hand to reconcile peoples who were enemies for a long time.

In the spirit of good will, he has achieved extraordinary results in creating the prerequisites for peace in Europe. Political and military détente between East and West Europe are a precondition of peaceful developments.

The Committee attaches importance to the fact that Willy Brandt both as foreign minister of the Federal Republic of Germany since 1966 and Federal Chancellor from 1969 onwards has taken definite steps to achieve such a détente. The Committee points to the signing of the agreement on the non-proliferation of nuclear weapons and the agreements with Poland and the Soviet Union renouncing force. Furthermore, the Committee remembers his endeavours to guarantee the basic rights of personal security and freedom of movement for the population of West Berlin.

Willy Brandt regards the strengthening of cooperation in Western Europe as an integrating part of a peace plan for the whole of Europe. With regard to strengthening the economic and political unity of Western Europe, the Federal Chancellor has also taken important initiatives.

The Nobel Committee regards this work as a whole as a fundamental contribution towards strengthening the possibilities for a peaceful development not only in Europe, but also in the world as a whole.

Foreword

After the war, Willy Brandt began his political work in Germany as representative of the Party Executive of the Social Democratic Party of Germany with regard to the Allies in Berlin; hence, in that city, the name of which has been linked so often with decisive political events during the past 25 years. Let us mention only three catchphrases: air lift, building of the Wall and Berlin negotiations. Here in Berlin, political developments are reflected in the everyday lives of the people as in no other place in the world. There was indeed no other city in the world which could have offered a politician a more constructive task, who made his most salient duty that of implementing and upholding peace in Europe and in the world.

Peace policy is to a great extent a policy of international agreements, a policy of balanced troop reduction and of armaments reduction. That also applies to German peace policy. But, German peace policy is — after all that has happened — also a question of political and human credibility. In this, it is not only a matter of what political content this peace policy has, it is also a matter of the form which it finds, it is a matter of the people who champion this policy. The people at the top as well as the electors and the members of the parties which support this policy.

Willy Brandt was awarded the Nobel Peace Prize. The honour went to the politician and the human being, Willy Brandt, to a German Federal Chancellor and to the Chairman of the Social Democratic Party, who has expressed time and again the humane components of politics in an exemplary manner.

Alfred Nau
Chairman of the Friedrich-Ebert-Stiftung

Contents

The Governing Mayor of Berlin

Coexistence and Development Aid

Excerpts from two lectures delivered to Harvard University in Cambridge, Massachusetts/USA on October 2nd and 3rd, 1962.

True coexistence is today the only alternative to atomic war and thus to the suicide of mankind. As we want to uphold world peace, more still, win it, we must make coexistence our own real cause in the consciousness of everybody. We must tear away from Khrushev and his propaganda the concept of coexistence which he has stolen from democracy and which he abuses as a disguise for his aggressive policy of crises.

True coexistence is a longterm test of our intellectual, political, economic and also military vital power. This task of implementing true coexistence causes Western democracy to be faced with a great test, the greatest test it has had to stand up to in history hitherto. In view of the Soviet pressure, we shall not only have to ward off the catastrophe and assert ourselves. This defensive task may not hypnotize us and lay claim to our whole attention. For the East-West conflict is not the only problem and basically not even the most important one we have to solve, if we want to win the future.

The technical and social upheavals which are going on at present all over the globe for everyone to see will probably be more decisive for the future and the progress of humanity. It is a truly revolutionary time in which we are living.

The progressive technicalization of the world has in it chances never known before and also dangers never known before. We must succeed in mastering the social effects of modern technology and in helping man to make purposeful use of the achievements of our age.

The peoples who have become independent in the parts of the world still to be developed require our support. They not only need money or equipment or experts — as important as these are. It is just as important for us to give them an example of living democracy by means of our progressive tackling of the problems. Our concept of coexistence is thus not limited to the relationship between the democratic West and the Communist East. It covers just as much the relationship between the rich and the poor peoples. Coexistence in our sense embraces the world.

If we stare at the East-West contrast as if under a spell, then we are in danger of seeing the development of the world distortedly. Western democracy with its values of personal freedom in a pluralist society has good chances not only of existing, but also of winning the future. We must find the energy to develop society further creatively and to allow as many single people as possible to have a part in the achievements of our civilization.

We are faced with an acid test of our maturity, of our vital force and of our ability to achieve solidarity. We cannot pass this test alone as individuals or as an isolated nation. We can only pass it in partnership.

In the last ten years, the political world map has experienced greater changes than during the whole period since the independence of the United States. And the face of our world in the future will change even more markedly than hitherto.

Since the birth of Christ, the population of the world has increased by some 2,500 million people. In the few decades to the year 2000, the rise is likely to total some 3,500 million people. In the 35 years in front of us, it will be larger than during the 1962 years which lie behind us. The population law will only gradually come into its own in the industrial societies growing up and apply a brake to the growth in population. In 2000, a little more than 1,000 million people are likely to be living in those areas which we call the Western world today. 2,500 million people in each case will be living in those areas under Communist rule today or those which we call the developing countries. That is a breathtaking prospect.

Hunger prevails in many parts of our earth. The explosion of population figures which, as indicated, does not die down until the industrial society will make the struggle to achieve the foodstuffs minimum a dominating topic in the years which lie before us. Mankind has today the means to produce enough food. We have shown that foodstuffs production can be increased more quickly than the growth in population. The investigations of UNESCO and internationally respected scientists have revealed that there are enough reserves on our globe to feed ten times as many people as are alive today.

It is not simply a matter of conscience, as to whether we can sleep peacefully, as long as children somewhere in the world regard a proper meal as a luxury and millions are threatened with starvation. It is also a matter of the political question, as to whether we are aware that to be or not to be of the Western world depends on development in the countries of need. We are not safe against downfall, if we succeed in averting the atomic catastrophe. The world will not be safe until thousands of millions of people forge a link with the progress of the modern industrial society before the year 2000. We know that a vacuum attracts all possible elements, who want to fill it up. The earlier categories of the yellow, the black and the white man are no longer applicable for this revolutionary process. It is here a matter of the process between rich and poor. Between those favoured by destiny and those who had to leave the gruesome paradise of untouched primitiveness and were never able to return there. Even if Communism did not exist, mankind would be faced with the dangers of a worldwide social explosion.

The East-West problem has for years been influenced by a North-South problem. One day, it may even be superimposed by it. In this case, however, the Soviet Union is an industrial power just like the United States. The more the Soviet Union stresses its economic development and its technical successes, all the greater and all the more similar will be the demands of the developing countries on it as well.

We cannot here follow the conflicts of interests, which have emerged in a number of developing countries between the Soviet Union and Communist China. But, I should like to underline the extent to which the world of the developing countries is following the race which is going on between China and India.

During this race of the two Asian population giants, a decision will be taken as to whether the democratic system of India modelled on the Western example leads further than the "Mao" method. It is our task to help India as much as possible. But it does not need to disrupt the interests of the West, if the Soviet Union becomes involved as well and invests its abilities.

In Africa, Communist influence is retrograde, but this, too, can change. Experience shows us clearly, however, that these countries are not served with an export of economic forms of private capitalism. Of necessity new, more marked combinations of planned economy and market economy arise, new variations of a "mixed economy."

In Latin America, we are following with great attention the efforts of the United States to achieve an alliance of progressive elements. There, too, better cooperation, with Western Europe included, could exercise a positive influence on the way taken by matters.

In the last years, the development aid of the West was ten times larger than that of the Communist East, that is in terms of money. The developing countries know that. It is certain that these countries must be industrialized despite the further development of their agriculture. Raising the standard of living without industry is impossible. The standard of living and education are the keys for getting the population explosion under control and preventing an explosion against the developing countries.

The obligation to feed starving people, the obligation to reduce the gap between the standard of living in the North and in the South, the obligation to help these nations to find their own way will have as a result

1. coexistence as peaceful rivalry will go on in these countries above all and
2. these countries will obtain increasingly their own force and their own power.

It will be neither an American nor a Soviet century, when we look back in 2000.

We are at the beginning of world history in the truest sense of the word. World history is no longer European-American history. Nobody should believe that that which is past can be revived with the practicable words of a third force. The new force will be represented by the large number of those, who with an increasing weight of their own do not want to accommodate themselves quite simply in the one camp or the other, and who will probably contribute towards changing both camps.

Coventry — Symbol of Hope in a Better World

Opening speech on April 24th, 1965 for the John F. Kennedy House in the British city of Coventry.

With humility and pride, I have accepted the invitation of the provost to come to Coventry and to speak at the opening of the John F. Kennedy House. Coventry and Kennedy are for everyone significant words, and particularly for the Mayor of Berlin.

No German can ignore the fact that his country is connected with the destruction of the city of Coventry and its large and beautiful cathedral. The word Coventry symbolizes the consequences of hatred and gruesome waging of war. And yet Coventry, just like a miracle, is also a symbol of hope in a better world.

The new cathedral of Coventry is recognized all over the world as a church of reconciliation.

It was President Kennedy who captured the imagination of young people all over the world and animated it. He gave the young generation the hope that peace and understanding can exist among the nations, among people. Linked with a remarkable realism, he saw new horizons and made them visible to other people. His sudden death made clear to very many young people the work had begun and it must be completed. Only a few days ago, I visited the family of the deceased President, and I extend to you their most cordial regards.

It would have been unimaginable twenty-five years ago to expect Coventry to become a world centre of reconciliation. It was at the time just as unimaginable that a Berliner, who insisted on remaining anonymous, a man who lost his whole family in an airraid on Berlin, would fit out this International Centre in Coventry, that Bishop Dibelius would open this International Centre and young Germans would help to complete it.

And yet that is exactly what happened, a new spirit has emanated from Coventry. It is a spirit which strengthens confidence in the better characteristics of human beings and in the chances for a life in freedom and good fortune. This spirit is also revealed in a convincing manner by the human ties between Coventry and Dresden in the other part of Germany.

The world needs this kind of spirit. We know today that it would be technically possible to solve the material problems of the world, of the nations and the human race. Science and technology make commonsense solutions possible, but the problem exists of mobilizing the intellectual power to solve our difficulties.

John F. Kennedy knew that and in the few years of his presidency, he displayed an intellectual power which can still be felt in many parts of a divided world. His life and his deeds gave young people all over the world a new consciousness of aim.

His dynamic energy and the spirit of reconciliation of Coventry should make this John F. Kennedy House a real centre of inspiration. I hope that many young people from my own country will have a part in this work and will contribute towards it. Today in a few weeks, my fellow-countrymen will remember and be reminded of this period of German history, which ended with the unconditional capitulation of May 1945.

But please remember: boys and girls who were born in 1945 will be voting this year for the first time in their lives. More than 55 percent of the present population were not consciously aware of National Socialism in Germany. Our young people realise more and more that they were born into the history of their country, and yet I believe that it would be unfair to make these young Germans responsible in the same way as my own generation and that of their grandfathers.

I believe it would accord with the spirit of Coventry to seize the outstretched hands of the young Germans. Justified and understandable scepticism should be restricted to those of us who prefer to look towards the past — what we should do from time to time for many reasons.

Certain people perhaps regard it as inappropriate for a German to talk about things of this kind here. I am convinced that Coventry which experienced the horrors of war and has brought about the wonderful spirit of reconciliation is the best place to talk about the problems of the younger generation. Both from the intellectual as well as the practical standpoint, it would be unwise to postpone active cooperation too long, until the last memories of a dreadful past have disappeared.

All of us, and particularly the younger generation are faced with tremendous tasks. If their hopes are to be fulfilled — their hopes in a world where everybody can live together in peace —, then much more than only good will is necessary.

We all know that in many areas of the world starvation and deficiency still prevail, and as long as there are still people starving, mankind may not rest content. Within the next ten years, the population of the earth will increase tremendously and the problem of feeding these people is not the only serious problem, with which we are faced. But up to now, people have still not realised sufficiently that the existence of the whole world depends on the future development of the countries and people in need.

I wish that many young people might stand up to this crucial test. They should not only understand things, but also act.

We are not sure that we shall survive, even if we succeed in avoiding a nuclear catastrophe; and even if there were no kind of dictatorship in the world, the world is faced with a worldwide social explosion. For many years, the East-West problem has been influenced by a North-South problem. One day, not all too distant, this order will perhaps be overthrown . . .

We can summarise the hopes and responsiblities, if we change President Kennedy's words a little: "Do not ask what the future will bring you; ask yourselves what you can contribute to a better future for mankind." With the help of God, may this spirit inspire the work of the John F. Kennedy House in Coventry.

We Must Struggle for Europe

Lecture at a conference of the Friedrich-Ebert-Stiftung on the subject of "European Community in the Atlantic Area" in Berlin during October 1963.

In the course of these two days, outstanding men who feel themselves committed to European unity and the Atlantic partnership have spoken here.

In the one way or the other, they are all the constructors of the Europe of tomorrow. In his way, each of them has announced his belief in the need for a real European community. Not only because of the shortterm interest in a strategy of defence, but also because of the greater interest in a strategy of peace. And every speaker has recognized explicitly or tacitly here that some form of communal political order is necessary. In other words, each of those who spoke before me was apparently aware that economic unity, too, can only have lasting success, if there is political progress.

The Friedrich-Ebert-Stiftung has rendered a service by putting on this congress and thus bringing together so much European experience under one roof. We have learnt a great deal through this congress. The obstacles which face us on the way to union have been clearly outlined. Sometimes with the conviction that they will be overcome. Sometimes with the concern that they could remain in existence for a long time. And sometimes with the scarcely concealed resentment that new obstacles are being continuously created unnecessarily. It is quite certain that no one here believes that everything is well with the European Community. Nobody here makes the attempt to nourish illusions. We feel rather obliged to destroy wishful thinking.

This conference could not have the purpose of developing a new formula for the union. It seems to me rather that we met here to find a formula for something else — for an attitude and a procedure which might serve to stop the growing disunity and to get the European ship into free water again.

I should like to make four statements about this:

1. The existing foundations for the greater unity to be created may not sustain further damage. That applies to Brussels, Luxemburg and Strassburg.

2. We may not allow the groups of states of free Europe to return to antiquated rivalries and cause the danger of economic civil wars.

3. The Europe coming into being may not regard itself as primarily being directed against others. On the contrary, it must be

At the traditional proclamation of the German Trade Unions' Congress on the 1st May in front of the reconstructed Reichstag building in Berlin, Willy Brandt, the Governing Mayor of West Berlin, spoke every year concerning the situation of the divided city and of its working people.

The visit of the President of the United States of America, John F. Kennedy, on 26th June, 1963 became a high point in the postwar history of Berlin.

Numerous trips took Mayor Willy Brandt to the United States. In talks with leading politicians and other leading personalities in public life he sought to win sympathy and support for Germany's divided capital city. Brandt met the future Nobel Peace Prize winner, Martin Luther King, in Washington.

The Mayor also devoted his attention constantly to the problems of the developing countries. He was certain that there could be no peaceful status quo between the nations as long as the deep division between rich and poor, ignorant and educated continued to exist in the world. In the picture Brandt is with the Indian politician, Mrs. Vijaya Lakshmi Pandit, in Berlin.

prepared in the shaping of a lasting peace to cooperate on a worldwide scale and liberally.

4. The temptation of anti-Americanism is something we should not succumb to. We need Atlantic partnership and must help to implement it.

It cannot be disputed that European unity has now lain on ice for almost a year. The radiant optimism of yesterday has become dulled. Hope in a comprehensive political framework has to a large extent been replaced by desperation. The power of imagination and the enthusiasm which created the Treaty of Rome and hence the Common Market appear to be paralysed. Where once confidence and promise prevailed, there is now doubt and mistrust in the air.

Let me put it to you in brutal frankness. A polluted haze lies over Europe. In many places, they are already saying that the Common Market is not only sick, but in reality it has been dead since January this year. In the view of these Cassandras, the persistent activity in Brussels is comparable with the twitching of muscles in a corpse before stiffening sets in. And there is no shortage of gravediggers, waiting eagerly to do business. I am convinced that they will wait for a long time in vain. We are referring here after all not to any old general store. The Common Market has its difficulties, but is by no means on its last legs. It is today still the greatest partner in world trade. Its economic growth lies higher than in most other industrial countries. Third states are in large numbers striving to become associated with the Common Market or to come to agreements with it. Stimulating achievements continue to radiate into the world from the intellectual and political energies of Europe. The moral, intellectual and physical forces which can be shown to exist have not however been used properly or adequately.

There are experts who know better than me about the inadequacy of the EEC and who have told us what must happen today and tomorrow. Here, it is a matter of better procedures, increased ability to react, accelerated decision-taking and greater possibilities for democratic control and co-shaping.

Here it is a matter above all as well of those careful consultations and pragmatic small jobs which are not to allow the distance between the EEC and EFTA to develop into a gap. For the next period of time, it is imperative for the door to be kept open for talks between the EEC and the EFTA partners to utilize the EEC as a bridge between "the Six" and Britain and the Council of Europe to be revived as a platform for forming will.

But, we know today better than in earlier times: The implementation of Europe cannot only be a technical procedure, but will have to be above all a human development. The EEC, too, will only regain its élan, if movements and forces become discernible for a Europe which has thicker and more far-reaching roots than those of economic or military purposefulness.

It is a question of not capitulating in the face of the difficulties nor of resigning because of the many special interests. It is a question of not losing sight of the goal of a larger solution comprising area and content and of not leaving it even in our day to day work.

If Europe wants to be politically and economically viable, if it wants to achieve self-determination for each of its components as well as Europe as a whole, if it wants to play its role in the world and promote progress, then we should not leave the way to greater unity.

We must move forward, even if we are urged to change course. Without consideration for where the pressure may come from. We may not allow ourselves to be diverted from our aim, quite regardless of what we are told. In other words, we must resist quo ante all tendencies in the direction of a European status. We must struggle for Europe, if we want to continue to exist in the next decade. To say nothing of the coming century.

Life in the free part of our continent is influenced by conflicting interests. A whole packet of political and economic elements is at work here. That is not always a bad thing. But, sometimes it appears as if the clock has stood still. And some act as if it was not necessary to give appropriate answers to the changes and challenges of our time.

Today, there exists no particular body which could speak on behalf of Europe with legal authority. And when I refer to "Europe," then I also mean Britain and Scandinavia.

I advocate explicitly such a gradation of political cooperation, through which the non-aligned status of Austria, Sweden and Switzerland receives consideration.

We may hope, too, that the peoples of the Iberian peninsula find their way to democratic cooperation, and that they will be represented in the assemblies of the Continent which is becoming united.

We should think logically beyond the limits of power policy, which cause clefts in this part of the world. Responsibly developed forms run without illusion of economic and cultural communication with the East European states are on the agenda. I hope that it will not remain there. We should try to expand the sphere of working together and fill it out reasonably.

But what we have to occupy us here and now above all is our own task as citizens of democratic states. It is our immediate problem to reawaken the dynamic forces, from which the earlier developments right through to the Common Market emerged.

In the first postwar years, we experienced an unplanned but effective interplay between the progressive ideas of the great Europeans and the pressure of active groups among the peoples. It was the time when the young people tore down the frontier barriers and united closely at the turnpikes. It was the time of demonstrations and mass rallies on behalf of Europe. It was this pressure from below which contributed to the fact that certain things happened above. That which has since been created and introduced is now in danger. Through new pressure from below, this danger can be averted. The European will of the peoples must be made visible again.

Strassburg, Luxemburg and Brussels have already brought important things for Europe, those which must be taken for granted. Approval and support of these are for me self-evident prerequisites for solving our problems intellectually and politically. But now it is a matter of mobilizing public opinion and down-to-earth thinking for the task of comprehensive and profound unity.

A Europe, the single parts of which do not work together purposefully and powerfully, economically and politically does not produce even the illusion of strength. A Europe, the member states of which have lost confidence in each other and hope in a common future, must inevitably lose the confidence of its allies and the respect of its opponents. Those who have no trust in themselves can only attract further, additional mistrust.

The retrogressive development must be stopped. And at the same time new steps forward must be prepared. It is a good thing that the new Federal government said a few days ago in Bonn that it would direct all its efforts towards achieving progress by means of new activity in the political shaping of Europe. I hope very much that it does not stop at this announcement.

Furthermore, I agree with the Federal Chancellor, when he wants to make the Franco-German treaty useful for the goal of shaping politically a greater Europe. But that requires, if one is consistent, German initiative.

The work of reconciliation between France and Germany has historical significance and an indisputable value of its own. But Franco-German friendship is no end in itself. We pay tribute to the men whose names are linked with this significant step. But it is not alone a matter for them, but for all of us to decide about the further steps. We pay tribute to greatness, but we may not allow ourselves to be intimidated by it. We should built upon it. That which has been created is not a monument.

Europe must derive new force from the dynamism of democratic initiative. It will not grow with the media of Cabinet policy of past times. In the age of nuclear weapons, not only generals can decide about this, it is true.

The logically most simple would doubtless be for Europe to become united in a federation by means of a parliament formed from the results of general and free elections. But that cannot be realized either today or tomorrow.

Today and tomorrow, we are concerned with three points:

1. The Coal and Steel Community and Euratom should be amalgamated with the EEC to form a unified whole;
2. the influence of the existing parliamentary bodies should be strengthened and
3. the democratic working together of peoples and citizens should be actively developed.

Europe can only exist as the result of voluntary cooperation. As the work of people who are conscious of their responsibility for each other. Responsibility for a cause which brings to a common denominator national interests with common European interests. From this responsibility and this common interest results the fact that the possibility of democratic arbitration is required. The old idea and practice of arbitration, which has authority over the various parts can perhaps help us further in Europe.

We must reach understanding about a new kind of sovereignty, which does not blot out the old sovereignties, but superimposes them in clearly defined fields. Thus, we must find the way which signifies less than political integration and more than the mere cooperation of governments.

That which is great and genuine in national feeling must grow and flourish. That applies to cultural connections, that culture in which we are rooted, love of our homeland and concern about our integrity. But, we must separate ourselves from that which is obsolete and damaging. That applies to everything which makes us blind to responsibility which we have to bear for others. That is something we must dispose of and learn to forget.

I am not using polemic against the expression of the Europe of the fatherlands. But I should like to expand it and say that the fatherlands of Europe should recognize Europe as their fatherland and make it such.

We want please never to forget that decisive impulses and contributions to Europe emanated from France. Some French names will never be forgotten in the history of European unity as such. I cannot imagine a Europe without France. I can just as little imagine Europe without England or without Germany. But also not a Europe under the dominating influence of one particular country. It would not be in accordance with reality to expect for the near future a supra-national state of Europe. But, we cannot get away from the summarizing of government authorities. In the meantime, we must subordinate ourselves to the repeated test of a less binding relationship. The content is more important than the form. It is not a matter of a Europe which is enough for itself. It is a matter of a Europe that is clear about its place in the world. And with that, we have reached the Atlantic partnership. That is to say that free Europe must join forces with America.

It is European spirit in which the proud saying on the American coat-of-arms is anchored: ex pluribus unum. The still magnificent thought picture of Aristotle, whereby the whole is more than the sum of its parts, should be an obligation and an orientation for the best spirits of our continent.

More than once, the United States through its presidents has invited Europe to have a part in Atlantic partnership on the basis of equal rights. Only a few months ago, President Kennedy again extended his hand to us here in Germany. He said: if the United States was striving for hegemony in Europe, then it would not support European union.

It is not a question of a satellite relationship with the United States. But we can only be true partners the way things are, if we approach together the powerful friend. We shall not be able to play an important role as a collection of many nice, small, national entities. Only a Europe which speaks with one voice and acts with a common will can appear on the scene as a world power. Hitherto, no suitable reply has followed on the American offer. No answer which might be regarded as binding for Europe. Those who rejected this offer as unacceptable were not speaking on Europe's behalf. Neither an individual, nor a group, nor a single country is empowered to take such a decision.

We owe the United States a reply which reflects a maximum of agreement of the intellectual and historical whole. Perhaps, this answer will not be of the kind which the United States would like to hear. But the cause demands more than single replies from Paris, London and Bonn. Washington should know where free Europe stands.

Atlantic partnership and the process of European union are simultaneous aims of equal status. The one may not wait for the other.

The same applies to the topical and in any case lively discussed question of nuclear armament. Let me say this here. It is right and necessary for Europe to have important influence on nuclear strategy and full access to the peaceful utilization of nuclear energy. But it is not necessary and — as I think — worth striving for that Europe should contribute towards the dissolution of the authority of decision about the nuclear deterrent. This authority should as part of partnership remain with the president of the United States. In connection with partnership, we must cooperate with the handicapped, not always "young" nations of this world, in Africa, in the Middle East and in Asia. A united Europe and a continent seriously striving for union might well do great things to render more effective aid than today to help towards self-help.

A whole host of African states has become associated with the EEC. But Europe is still in danger of becoming regarded by the new nations as an economic power centre of a negative kind. And yet, there is not the slightest doubt that a more closely linked Europe would be in a position to implement a development programme of a completely new kind. A programme which in relation to the Marshall Plan could certainly assert itself. A Europe in the process of progressive union could in fact do a great deal

to uphold the build-up of the OECD,

to increase aid for the developing countries collectively and bilaterally,

to facilitate the levelling off of the balance of payments and

to control in a commonsense manner the expanding East-West trade.

I am speaking here not only as Berlin Mayor and not primarily as a man of my party, but above all as a European from Germany. The persistent division of Europe constitutes in my way of thinking just as much a danger as the unnatural division of Berlin. My people will be able to tolerate the situation of this country and this city as long as the hope exists that the heavy burden must not be carried always. It will be for this people a criterion for a right or wrong solution of the European question, whether its excludes, permits or favours the reunification of Germany.

Only the plenary assembly of European states, the morally political force of which is recognized by Moscow and is confirmed by the partner on the other side of the Atlantic can offer convincing security guarantes. And only if all our neighbours and all their neighbours accept these guarantes, can the German people reckon with having a part with equal rights and as a whole in the opportunities of this historical period. I do not believe that Germany's hopes can die. They are at one with the hopes of Europe. As a European, I call on that being done at last which is necessary.

That the available means be utilized in order that the latent possibilities of our community may become reality.

We have indeed no time to lose. The longer the Europeans squabble with each other, the less they will have to say to both the United States and the Soviet Union about the shaping of the Europe of tomorrow. And all the less necessary it will be for Russia or America to listen to what Europe has to say.

The Europeans who expect bad things from the talks between Washington and Moscow should bring to an end their fainthearted lack of self-assertion. They should have confidence in themselves and their cause.

We may not move apart just at that moment when the Soviets and the Americans are about to move closer in certain spheres. When Moscow and Washington speak about the possibilities of partial understanding, then we of course expect to be consulted at every important stage. We are prepared to help, whenever it a question of a realistic rapprochement and detente, but just as obviously we must insist on our inviolable rights. We want to do here as well what is necessary. We should be able to do it with the authority and in the name of the European community, which has committed itself to the peaceful development of mankind.

Anyone who has made my acquaintance will know that I am not speaking the words of a third force from the world of imagination of past ages. I am speaking about a political community which has its roots in intellectual values and in that united moral force which grows up out of the will and the hope of human beings. It is not a matter only of the decisions of governments. It depends also on the people themselves. To quote a few examples:

Are the youth associations prepared to appeal to the young generation more emphatically than in the past years to cooperate in the Europe of tomorrow?

Are the trade unions prepared to offer their influence to mobilize broad sections of those in factories and offices on behalf of Europe?

Are the mayors prepared to expand the partnerships between the municipalities and put them in the service of an active European policy?

Are the universities prepared to make their irreplacable contribution to a kind of Council of Intellectual Europe?

Our governments should not believe that the enthusiasm for Europe has become extinguished. The will of the peoples to achieve European unity could easily be awakened again. And it must be awakened, so that it becomes recognized. The peoples of Europe want to see deeds.

The new call is that the new initiative should emanate from here. Germany had to be modest after the war and had to be grateful for a chance to cooperate. Today, 18 years later, there can no longer be any misunderstanding, when the call to unite Europe comes from Berlin, the call to the peoples and the statesmen. Our old continent has men who are farsighted and able enough to continue the process of union. Many of them are working in European organizations. They are the executors of a great idea and an historical necessity.

In these last two days, we did some stocktaking. I have tried to make clear the way we must take. My earnest and urgent appeal goes to all those who are called upon to lead us out of the European cul-de-sacs. They must help to clear aside the obstacles which lie in our way.

The people in Europe want Europe. I am convinced that if we call the people, they will reply.

About the National Self-Image of the Germans

Speech made at the award of an honorary doctorate by the New School for Social Research in New York on April 19th, 1965.

In the life of the individual just as in the life of the peoples, only too often the comfortable, the easier paths are trodden, although the comfortable paths are not always the right ones. It is a good thing to take the uncomfortable path in particular when it is the right one. The award which you have made to me today is an honour. I think I can show my gratitude best, if I tell you something about how I see the situation of my people today. I shall do so in the spirit of sincerity which is not always comfortable. A plea and an appeal will derive their origins from this. Twenty years have passed since the end of the Second World War. The Germans have worked hard. In the larger part of their country, where they received the chance to do this, they have created very stable democratic institutions. But, as a people, they have not found their peace. Their national question is not solved.

Germany is divided. The one part, the Federal Republic, has become a powerful economic power. Its military strength is also presentable, but limited and conventional and subordinate to NATO. A Communist regime has been imposed upon the other part, the Soviet occupied zone, and this has also been relatively successful economically for some time, revealing growing self-assertion. Berlin was held despite all the attempts to squeeze out the three powers which have become friends and allies. The Berliners have remained firm and have not allowed themselves to be led astray.

Twelve million people, i. e. more than 20 % of the population of the Federal Republic, are refugees or expellees. They have been integrated practically in society. In West Germany, there is no rightwing or leftwing radical political movement to be taken seriously. 55 percent of the Germans living today no longer experienced the Nazis consciously. Among the young people, as well as among the older ones, interest is growing in the questions after reunification. Those are the facts which constitute my point of departure. May 8th will awaken memories. The terror which spread across the world in the abused name of the Germans will come alive again. The peoples cannot forget this chapter of their recent history. And why should they? One can only learn from history, if one knows it. But I should not be surprised, if the German people as well finds it difficult to achieve clarity about the worst chapter of its history.

33

I have never shared the illusions of certain people who believe that one has to let the grass grow over matters. I can say here, as I have often said in Germany, that it is crass opportunism to want to solve problems by letting them lie. Memory cannot be extinguished by the statute of limitations, and I regret profoundly that the wrong impression has come about that the Federal Republic not so long ago took certain decisions only under the pressure of world opinion. These decisions were solely the result of the country's own conviction, and that is how things had to be. That has something to do with pride and no people can live without pride. That applies also to the Germans, and certain aspects of this are now apparent. I have read with great concern the disquieting questions which have been put in many places and also in the United States, whether we are at the eve of a wave of nationalism in Germany. That is not the case. I am not overlooking here a series of irresponsible statements and dubious activities. But what we are concerned with in reality looks like this to me. For the space of twelve years the German people were excessive in their nationalism. The total claim to hegemony was followed by the total downfall. The result was that, alongside many others, national consciousness became a negative quantity, a minus unit in the life of Germany. In the constitution, the possibility was created of transferring sovereignty to supranational organs. An integrated Europe became the goal, where certain of my fellow-countrymen hoped to find their greater homeland. The economic growing together of Europe is making progress. The political union, the United States of Europe, which take over and unite the sovereignty of the nations, does not lie on the writing desks of the statesmen and is not on their calendars as a task of today or tomorrow or as some date in the near future.

We should not become resigned as a result. We must strive for qualified political cooperation among the six countries of the Common Market. We must bring about agreements between the Common Market and the Free Trade Zone. We must keep the door open to the peoples and the states of Eastern Europe in the possible forms of communication today or tomorrow.

But quite independently of these efforts, it was and is just as inevitable as the rising of the sun tomorrow again that the German people is asking about its national identity. It would have been inevitable, too, without the self-willed call of General de Gaulle for a Europe of the fatherlands. In any case, he accelerated this development. Who can be surprised, if the people in divided Germany also are asking about their fatherland which is larger than the Federal Republic. In this connection, the question, "Why only de

Gaulle?" should surprise nobody. It would perhaps not be necessary to remember what John F. Kennedy said in Berlin: "In 18 years of peace and of tested reliability, this generation of Germans has earned the right to be free, including the right to see reunited in lasting peace families and the nation, in goodwill towards 'everybody'."

These 18 years have now become 20, but the right of self-determination has not become reduced and the call for self-determination resounds more loudly. We say 20 years are enough, precisely for reasons of human rights and because of the cause of peace. We say that also when we know that still unforeseeable difficulties stand in the way of fulfilling this right. Even if we know that alongside the responsibility of the Four Powers there is a German responsibility. And we say it knowing only too well that peace is on a higher plane than any national goal. It will be the task of German policy in the next few years to ensure that the national consciousness of the German people finds its balance. The fact that after excess and negation the true measure of national feeling will be found, which is free from arrogance and is borne by good will with regard to all peoples and all nations. Whether it is successful will be the real decision about the fate of democracy in Germany. None of the democratic parties in the Federal Republic may avoid this responsibility. If they were to fail in the face of this, if they were not to grasp the national self-image, if they were to let the flag sink which blows for the right of self-determination, then, and only then could they arise to forge the weapons of radicalism out of the national feeling of disappointment. There is not a nationalist wave in the Federal Republic. Naturally, there are incorrigibles, those who never add to what they have learned and never change or those who readjust themselves too often and too quickly. No people is ever free from this. But decisive is the determining, healthy process of a people's convalescence, of a people which, just like any other, cannot live in the longterm without pride in itself. It is my plea to have understanding for this.

Please remember that in Germany in the autumn those who were born in 1944 will vote for the first time. More than half of the German people regards itself with justification personally free from the responsibility of their fathers. We know that young people as well are born into the history of their people. But no one may demand of German sons that they bear responsibility for the Germany of their fathers. I know in any case from my sons that they would not like to assume the responsibility for everything in the way I do. There have never been so many young people in Germany who know foreign countries. Hundreds of thousands of them spend their holidays and many of them years of study beyond the country's frontiers, and there are millions of encounters with the youth of other peoples. Natural self-assertiveness without arrogance, scepticism with regard to their fathers, a factual approach towards the people of their age, those are the characteristics of German youth. Are those not the characteristics of young people almost all over the world? The critical observers also have never been able to detect a sign of nationalist arrogance in German youth or a sign of hate of other peoples. The young generation in my country would just as much like to travel to Russia and Poland as to France and Italy. That is encouraging.

Therefore, I say to my friends in America, and not only in America; I must protect my people against unjustified attacks. Germany needs their confidence, the confidence of its friends in the reliability of its word. At the same time we must endeavour to convince our present opponents that the Germans want to live in peace and friendship with all their neighbours. Unemburdened by the past, self-assertive and liberal, the young generation in Germany stretches out its hand to the youth of other peoples. This is my appeal to youth: do not reject the hand of our youth, because mistrust of the fathers has not yet died down. Presentday Germany deserves trust.

The Foreign Minister

Limiting the Arms Race and Making Peace More Secure!

Speech at the Conference of Non-Nuclear Nations in Geneva on September 3rd, 1968.

This hall has been witness to the many hopes and many disappointments of mankind between two World Wars. The hall is accomodating a conference which, with regard to its plan and goal, could today already be termed historic.

The reason for that is that here an overwhelming majority of the world's nations, inspite of differing political systems, societies and backgrounds, have assembled to work out areas of common interest. What unites us all is the will to renounce the atom as a weapon.

What unites us all is also the conviction that no disadvantage arising from this voluntary limitation of these weapons can affect our peoples, but that with this step, the peace and progress of humanity will be served.

This gathering may also be called historic because it vividly illustrates that it is not enough merely to ban the atomic bomb in order to fend off the threats to the independence and sovereign integrity of all nations. We cannot escape the consequences of this knowledge.

Those states that do not possess atomic weapons are interested in knowing how they can obtain more security. They want to be advised how to limit the arms race and bring it under some form of control in order to make peace more secure.

This is no academic theme. These tasks cannot be solved in a vacuum, but only in light of the realities of the world in which we live. Without trust in certain fundamental rules for the co-existance of States, there is no control of the destructive forces which atomic energy possesses. Without such trust there is no international order. Signatures mean nothing unless they are based on a modicum of reliability! Whoever possesses power, especially atomic power, does not necessarily have morality or wisdom on his side. I do not believe that it is the task of this conference to organise an unyielding resistance to those world powers which history has burdened with an enormous responsibility, a responsibility that I do not envy.

The great dangers for humanity are posed by the great powers — not by the small ones. In other words: what must be resolved is a definition of the responsibilities which the atomic powers must assume.

It would be sheer madness for us all to strive to achieve the same potential for destruction which the great powers possess. It is however, reasonable and necessary to strive to obtain that equality of rights and opportunities for all States, without which we could not face our peoples, our younger generation and history. The West German delegation is here for no other reason than to make its own constructive contribution. We offer our hand in the spirit of co-operative partnership for the peaceful exploitation of atomic energy. It is our wish to co-operate on the matter of security in order to bring positive results that much nearer to reality. Everyone in this hall knows that the threat of force and the fear of its use are no abstract questions. Everyone knows that whole nations fear for their independence and that there is deep anxiety concerning the future of mankind.

Whatever has been achieved since the Second World War in the way of norms of international relations, in restoring confidence, which even considering reverses seemed to have grown, is again brought into question.

Regardless of what one may understand as the sphere of interest of a nuclear power, it does not change the fact that the universal principles of international law, as they are stated in the United Nations Charter, thereby obtaining their binding expression and unconditional validity, may never be violated: sovereignty — territorial integrity — freedom from violence — the right of self determination — human rights. Guarantees for security, disarmament and prospects for the peaceful applications of atomic energy can only then be discussed with some hope of success if a common will and common proposals conform to the pressing need of the international community for international order.

It is only logical for one to assume that the particular form the here assembled nations will continue to adhere to in carrying out the work they have commenced will be dependent upon the course and result of this conference.

The Federal Republic of Germany has, in compliance with the wishes of its Allies, denied itself production of atomic weapons and accordingly subjected itself to international controls. The Federal Republic of Germany does not aim to achieve for itself any direct authority over atomic weapons and does not aim to possess them. It wishes to re-emphasise this position. Its security lies with an alliance. But at the same time, we share as one of the non-nuclear nations in making a demand for the exclusion of pressure and threat of force.

From the resolution of the United Nations Security Council on June 19th, 1968 and the related declarations of the nuclear powers, as well as from the exemption in the last sentence of the preamble to the Non-Proliferation Treaty, to a balanced security system is still a long way.

Let us look at it realistically: as long as nuclear weapons are not universally abolished, they can never be prevented from playing a role in the deterrent and collective defence forces of the world. Obviously it is not enough simply to outlaw nuclear aggression or the threat of nuclear aggression in the interests of the non-nuclear nations, and of their wish to continue their development in dignity and independently. Doubtless the introduction of conventional weapons by a nuclear nation could also endanger the independence of a non-nuclear nation; it might not even be necessary to make the threat of nuclear aggression. On that basis the demand has arisen that all nations should renounce the use of force with one another. And that means the non-nuclear nations, with regard to one another, as well as the nuclear powers in regard to the non-nuclear nations. The only legitimate exception would be the right to individual and collective self-defence according to Article 51 of the United Nations Charter.

For the relations between nations, only an outright ban on force, as contained in the United Nations Charter, can be effective as an encouragement to peace. It is therefore not permissable to limit the renunciation of force to certain States. As far as we are concerned, we would like to add that we do not approve of intervention by anyone.

The question then arises whether or not the important principle of the renunciation of force is not the starting point that the non-nuclear nations could take for a resolution or a convention concerning general security. The German delegation is ready to make its own proposals in this direction and to discuss pertinent proposals from other nations.

We shall strive to see that every aggression with nuclear, biological and chemical weapons, as well as the direct and indirect threat of such aggression, should be forbidden as a violation of the universally valid principle of non-violence, as laid down in the principles of Article 2 of the Charter of the United Nations. The renunciation of the use and threat of every form of pressure and violence that could threaten the territorial integrity and political independence of any State should be generally reiterated. The obligations of nations to carry out their international relations on the basis of the sovereign equality and the right to self determination of all peoples should be strengthened and conflicts should be settled peacefully. They should unite possible increased international co-operation with the goal of realising the principles of the ed Nations Charter in the areas of disarmament and armament control, and with that take a step towards freeing mankind from fear.

The Federal Republic of Germany has initiated a policy of trying to create a zone of relaxed tension in Europe which could serve as a step towards a permanent era of peace. It has proposed: reduced confrontation, mutual renunciation of force, normalisation of relations with the states of East and South-East Europe, regulated co-existence in Germany, easing of cultural, economic and scientific exchanges. These efforts have received a rude shock. However, we remain ready to work for a European zone of peaceful neighbourliness which will gradually lead to constructive fraternization in which dangerous confrontation can be reduced. Therefore we favour a balanced mutual reduction of troops with which an appropriate settlement of the problems of the nuclear weapons stationed in this region could be combined. In this regard there are certain points of contact with the famous Polish proposals. In December 1967 I pointed out to the German Bundestag that we are ready to start consultations on a treaty that would seek the step-wise reduction of nuclear weapons in all of Europe, co-inciding with a balanced reduction of all armed forces. This readiness still exists. I do not wish to conceal the fact that my government can only regard such security mearures as find their way into resolutions, declarations or conventions only as complimentary supports for its security in the present world situation. The world must succeed in reducing step-wise the basic causes for the insecurity of the non-nuclear nations, which means advancing towards real nuclear disarmament in connection with disarmament of the enormous nonconventional arms potential of the nuclear powers.

The nuclear powers have been called upon to take concrete steps. It is for us, the non-nuclear nations, to see to it that they do not escape their responsibilities and support negotiable proposals for possible solutions.

We should also set our sights on reducing certain delivery systems for nuclear warheads. If it should come to negotiating about intercontinental missiles, the reduction of other long distance missiles in all of Europe should be included in the discussion. While concerning ourselves with the threat of massive nuclear annihilation we should not forget that there are other weapons of massive annihilation whose effects could perhaps be graver — I am referring to the B and C weapons. In 1954, the Federal Republic of Germany renounced in an international treaty its right to produce not only atomic weapons, but also biological and chemical

42

weapons. We would welcome it if other nations took a similar step. The Geneva Protocol of 1925 failed to define what bacteriological and chemical weapons are. Perhaps in this regard the definition used in the German renunciation of production in 1954 could be of use. We offer our co-operation and support for all efforts, which, without discrimination, are directed towards a more effective rephrasing of the bans on bacteriological and chemical weapons, with the goal of removing mankind's fear of them.

An important task of this conference is to encourage the research, development and exploitation of nuclear energy for peaceful purposes.

Nobody and nothing should be allowed to hinder research and development in this respect. The government of the Federal Republic of Germany sees as significant the declaration that the American government made before the United Nations on May 15th, 1968. Also the security measures must be strict enough to prevent the misuse of fissionable materials for weapons purposes. The idea of instrumented inspection of the flow of fissionable materials at strategic points coincides with this goal. We in the Federal Republic of Germany are undertaking steps towards achieving a practicable realization of this concept. This work, which has also attracted the interest of the International Atomic Energy Organization is carried out in the Nuclear Research Center in Karlsruhe. We would like to give you the opportunity to become acquainted with this work at first hand. It is my pleasure, in the name of the Federal Republic of Germany, to invite all interested delegates to visit the Nuclear Research Center in Karlsruhe, where also the modern fast breeder reactor technique is being developed. Our nuclear activity takes place within the scope of the European Atomic Community. It has operated for more than ten years, an effective control system, which in conjunction with the verification treaty of the International Atomic Energy Organization, must remain intact.

Nuclear energy is one of the great hopes of all countries which suffer from a lack of energy sources. How else are they to fight the hunger of the masses which could become a catastrophe for all of mankind!

The Federal Republic of Germany intends to share the results of its work with all peoples. We are ready to strengthen international co-operation in nuclear research through expanded exchange of technical experience and information, through the participation of others in the programmes of German nuclear research centers and German research establishments, through stipendiums and the despatching of experts. In every possible way we would like to bring the numerous contacts already existing closer and establish new ones.

On September 10th, 1926, or 42 years ago, Gustav Stresemann made the speech with which he brought Germany into the League of Nations. Many of his demands still hold true today, the tasks incorporated in these demands remain to an extent unfulfilled. If today a German Foreign Minister eludes to them, he does so in the awareness of what a terrible price many peoples — and the German people itself — had to pay, because the warnings of Briand and Stresemann went unheeded. The German foreign policy is subject to many distortions and even slander. Mis-representations are something no one can entirely escape from, but I emphatically reject slander. I do this as someone whom no one can associate with the atrocities of Hitler, and who, in spite of that, bears his share of national guilt.

We learned from history. The Federal Republic of Germany consistently pursues a policy that seeks to replace a balance of terror with the reign of peace on this continent. There is no alternative to this.

The people in the Federal Republic of Germany have not pressed to be armed; our Bundeswehr is no national army, but is fully integrated into the North Atlantic Treaty Organization. Atomic weapons are stored on the soil of the Federal Republic of Germany, as you all know; but it is not we who have control of them, and we have no ambition to control them.

The government of the Federal Republic of Germany is determined to carry out its peace policy unperturbed, regardless of all the reversals which have occurred through no fault of this government. We not only have understanding for the wish of all nations to live within secure boundaries, but we also are ready to demonstrate this with words and deeds — without treaties, when they are not necessary, with treaties, when these can be of use.

The youth in many of our countries cannot understand why we, the older generation, cannot solve the problems of an age dominated by science. Not violence, only reason can supply youth with an answer.

This is not a speech which was conceived weeks ago. It was put together in the last few days, in spite of these last days. In central Europe there exists the greatest concentration of military destructive power in all of history. This is against all reason. It runs counter to the interests of all peoples. If others demonstrate their power and so give rise to new dangerous tensions, it cannot possibly be our responsibility to answer for the increase in tension. I see it as an opportunity, as a task, as a possibility for the non-nuclear nations which are gathered here to unite the force of their will, the force of their reason and the force of morality in one appeal to the nations and to responsible statesmen: let every nation determine its own path, for only then can the nations collectively best serve humanity, which has so many great and unsolved problems which remain to be dealt with.

Peaceful Co-Existence in the Spirit of Solidarity

Speech given at a UNESCO Conference on November 6th, 1968.

Peace is not only the absence of war and violence, although we know that there are peoples that today would even be grateful for that. Peace demands freedom from oppression, from hunger and from ignorance. Only under these conditions can men and peoples develop their capacities freely and responsibly.

A permanent and just peace requires that all peoples have equal chances for economic development. In this respect, UNESCO can function in an outstanding way. The Federal Republic of Germany should like to support this function in so far as it is in a position to do so.

What concerns us, as you already know, is the cultural advancement of individual countries. For a Foreign Minister however, it is of first importance to represent his country in foreign lands and international organisations, and this also holds true in questions of education and culture. I would like to say three things in regard to this responsibility.

1. We emphatically believe in the intellectual and moral solidarity that is called for in the preamble of the UNESCO Constitution.

2. We are especially concerned that the international dialogue should be methodically and objectively carried out. And, if I may be so immodest as to add that, besides the terrible and fateful errors of German history, the art of dialogue with people of other persuasions has been an excellent tradition in our intellectual development. Our literature and science both bear witness to this.

3. A whole series of concrete UNESCO projects deserve our special interest and active sympathy.

Peaceful co-existence demands the spirit of solidarity. It compels us to greater efforts in order to overcome egoism. This is the demand of the hour. And this demand is true for East and West as well as for North and South. Exaggerated nationalism and oppressed communities are forms of egoism that instead of enriching to co-existence of peoples, hold it back. They lead to injustifiable differences artificially contrived, and increase the distance between man and man and nation and nation.

Others have said it before me, but in spite of that I will say it again: if humanity is not to be confronted with new difficult and unavoidable dangers, the gap between rich and poor, between educated and ignorant, between the hungry and the well-fed must be closed. Only in this way can one create the secure peace of to-morrow. This battle is heroic, although it is not fought with tanks and guns.

UNESCO would not be doing its best if it had only to answer the question: how many divisions? It does better when one realises that in struggling to create the world of tomorrow, the distribution of knowledge has become a decisive weapon. Now, we all know from bitter experience that there is political illiteracy, intellectual immaturity and moral confusion that thrive even though men know how to read and write. But it still remains true that if people cannot even read and write, only in a very limited sense can they be considered as responsible citizens. Therefore it is good that UNESCO devotes great efforts to wiping out illiteracy.

It is equally important that the school and educational systems all over the world be improved. Our readiness towards achieving so-lidarity is more obviously challenged when it comes to the scien-tific and technological co-operation between the more advanced and less advanced nations. This co-operation must be energeti-cally encouraged. Really, the most important goal that UNESCO can have, can only be that of sharing and spreading knowledge. If UNESCO accomplishes the task of a world-wide equalization of knowledge, it will have served the cause of inviolable peace, which our peoples long for, with historic distinction.

Technological civilization is in a position to spread itself all over the earth. But simultaneously we see that young people in many places are rebelling against this civilization.

This is a process which has many unique features, but whose general tendencies cannot be concealed. One of the simplest of explanations is that youth longs not for that which was, but rather for that which could be. However, does this not also involve a fer-mentation directed against alienation and de-humanization? Be-hind the noisy protests does there not lurk the question of "free-dom for what"? Is it not being emphatically pointed out to us that material improvements and technical perfections are, in them-selves, not a goal? Is it not becoming more apparent hat political decision-making processes are less and less subject to easy clarafication, and have become ever more difficult to understand? Are we not confronted with the fear that man can be managed, that he can be degraded to the level of a controlled and pro-grammed robot?

No one among us should be told to consider these questions. It is really not so surprising that young people should be upset about the incongruity between obsolete systems and new possibilities; when they protest against the contradiction between appearance and reality and when they despair of policies which set-up noble goals, but prove themselves helpless against abridgement of rights, the use of force, oppression and bloodshed.

I am not in favour of lecturing to young people. I am against concessions to intolerance and violence. In these cases, our responsibility towards, and respect for those who follow us, compel us not to yield. But I believe we should not allow ourselves to become estranged. Listening is not enough. We must confront their challenge with a readiness to question ourselves, and to learn from it.

The fight for peace can only be won with the younger generation. It must be convinced that a world-wide peaceful co-existence can only be achieved if violence is banned as a means of political argument.

The general rejection without exception of the application of force or of threatening force belongs to the fundamental political thinking of the government which I represent. It was, therefore, only logical that at the Conference of Non-Nuclear Nations in Geneva we introduced a resolution favouring non-aggression and outlawing the use of force. To our satisfaction, the resolution was adopted by a large majority. I would like to emphasise here our readiness to clarify or eliminate, through peaceful negotiations with other governments, all outstanding differences.

The Federal Republic of Germany does not threaten anyone. It has, thereby becoming the first state in the world to do so, declined, in treaties with its Alliance partners, to produce all A, B and C weapons. It is positively engaged in paving the way towards a European peace, and has decided to participate in a mutually balanced disarmament. It is in agreement with all those that do not wish to see the elementary rights of a people violated. It would be ready to convert industrial capacities no longer required for arms production to peaceful and constructive uses. I believe that this is a perspective which, especially on the floor of the UNESCO building, should be appreciated.

We have been able to determine how similar the interests of our many states are — independent of their economic systems and of their geographic distance, when the security of their peaceful internal development and of their future prosperity is at stake. Among them are the interests of many states which are not world powers and which have no ambitions to become world powers, but which insist on their right to develop themselves freely and without concern and anxiety, and which do not seek to shirk their responsibility with and to the world. In the years to come I believe there will increasingly be such areas of common interest.

The former Foreign Minister of West Germany and Ambassador Schnippenkötter at the Conference of the Non-Nuclear Nations on 30th August, 1968 in Geneva.

The former Foreign Minister of West Germany, Willy Brandt, clarifies the European policies of the Federal Republic of Germany at a session of the Advisory Assembly of the Council of Europe in Strasbourg.

The Foreign Minister of West Germany held numerous talks with representatives of Third World nations. Above, our picture depicts him in conversation with Foreign Minister Patrick D. Anin of Ghana, and below with the Prime Minister of Malaysia, Tun Haji Abdul Razak.

Permanent Peace in Europe as the Goal

Lecture given at the annual meeting of the Advisory Board of the Friedrich-Ebert-Stiftung on November 30th, 1967 in Düsseldorf.

Unfortunately, I was unable to take part in the annual meeting of the Friedrich-Ebert-Stiftung in Hamburg last year. The decision of the two main parties to work together in a coalition Government for the stabilising of the state and the economy came at exactly that time. Then, it was of the utmost importance to bring order into the disorganized public finances, not to allow the economic recession to develop into a serious crisis, and to create the conditions for new economic growth. It was also necessary to fend off foreign dangers and to maintain the Federal Republic in a favourable position for foreign negotiations.

The foreign policy of the Government of the Grand Coalition has visibly brought together under one banner those who, a year ago, many still attempted to keep separate, although since 1945 they have really belonged together. I am referring to the fact that the fundamentals of the foreign policy of the Federal Republic of Germany have not only been established by Konrad Adenauer, Heinrich von Brentano, and Walter Hallstein. Men like Ernst Reuter, Wilhelm Kaisen, Max Brauer and Hans Böckler played no less a role in regaining confidence and trust in Europe and the world for Germany. Among those men who have added to Germany's standing belongs also the Chairman of the Social Democratic Party in the post-war years, Doctor Kurt Schumacher. Undeniably, he was the great opponent of Konrad Adenauer when the outlines of Federal German foreign policy were being formulated. Even so, as Doctor Adenauer's name is associated with the reconciliation with France, the creation of the European Coal and Steel Union, Western European unification, the admission of the Federal Republic of Germany to NATO, so is the name of Kurt Schumacher associated with the prevention of the communist compulsory unification of Berlin and the political viability of West Berlin, for the co-operation of the working classes in the Federal Republic from the very beginning and efforts towards harmonizing democracy with the concept of nationhood.

The contribution made by the German Social Democrats under the leadership of Erich Ollenhauer, Fritz Erler and others for state and nation also has its own importance. However, international developments independent of German foreign policy have made themselves forcefully apparent. Thus there is more than one reason why, in spite of the sometimes bitter conflicts concerning the course of German foreign policy, the two great parties never developed in completely diverging directions.

European Policy Aimed at Relaxation of Tensions and Mutual Co-operation

The objective realization of the current situation was strong enough to convince both parties to bury their longstanding enmity in order to preserve the Federal Republic of Germany in its present form and to secure for it, in the second phase of the post-war period, stability and future prospects.

When this present regime began its work, there were immediate alterations in the course of foreign policy. People who do not believe this statement require only to check the facts pertaining — if nothing had changed then certain people would not have felt it necessary to attack our foreign policy.

Occasional polemic can or should change the fact that German foreign policy has as its main goal the securing of a permanent peace. That holds true today just as it did one year ago. This means above all a European policy aimed at relaxation of tensions, mutual co-operation and unity. This also remains unchanged, and it will continue to be the position as long as I am Foreign Minister.

The European component has always enjoyed in German foreign policy thinking since the end of the Second World War a special consideration, not only from those who shaped official policy, but also from those who questioned this policy. This was very natural because the political landscape after 1945 had been radically altered.

Although realising the differences between the present international situation and that existing at the time of the Weimar Republic, the foreign policy of the Federal Republic of Germany is in many respects a continuation of policies associated with the names Friedrich Ebert, Walther Rathenau and Gustav Stresemann. The annual meeting of the Friedrich-Ebert-Stiftung offers a welcome forum to speak about the responsibility of the Germans towards Europe. The Social Democrat Friedrich Ebert strongly felt this responsibility, especially during his term as President. In the difficult period following November 1918 he was constantly preoccupied with the thought that Europe, although its peoples may have shortly before been deadly enemies, could not do without the contribution that the German people could make towards a peaceful world.

Trust in German Foreign Policy

In 1919, Ebert spoke of the German people having created "light and air" for themselves. They would make something of themselves "abroad" and at home, whereby he was certainly not referring to a new position of power for Germany in a "concert of nations," but rather to the ability of the German people after experiencing a world war to realize certain principles and that the European peoples would live with one another in peace with justice. "Regardless of how difficult a period our people have experienced, we shall never despair of their creative energies!" he said at the time. In the same speech before the Weimar Assembly on February 11th, 1919, he added: "We have solemnly renounced the principle of violence between nations. In its place we want justice and freedom to rule."

Peace, justice and freedom were these principles which Friedrich Ebert wanted to see brought out in the creative energies of the German people. Through them Germany would take its appropriate place and exercise a reasonable amount of influence in Europe. Friedrich Ebert did not want to see the careful and delicate foreign policy of the young Republic become inconsequent and insincere. Reestablishment of relations could only take place with the Western countries if the Government totally rejected any type of Machiavellian intrigues. The President was, above all, concerned with bringing about an atmosphere of trust and respect. Only from a definite position as a member of the Western countries would Germany orient itself to the historically necessary task of co-operation with the East.

Today's European Policy

The European policy which we are now concerned with did not just begin one year ago, not even twenty years ago. Its roots go even further back into the past. European thought played an important role in the past century in the development of European democracy. The fact that after the First World War men like Friedrich Ebert were not sufficiently heeded proved to be fateful not only for the German people, but for all of Europe. And as far as the period from 1933 to 1945 was concerned, with all its crimes and errors, one must, from the German point of view, conclude, no matter how difficult that may be, that what came out of Ebert's idealistic policy was the betrayal of Europe.

After 1945, the idea of European unity was hopefully taken up by the Geman people. Others were tempted occasionally to look on the impulse of our public opinion towards a European orientation as an escape into the future, and from out of our past. There was not a little truth in this. But it was probably closer to the truth to say that the future of the destroyed and divided German nation had to be carefully thought out.

At that time it was also thought that through a policy of European unity the terrible experiences of the past could be prevented from recurring — a thought that continues to influence our policy. This means co-operation instead of destructive rivalry; instead of the dominating position of a single state, the equality of all European nations. This envisages a co-operation and unity so binding that none of the parties could be able to initiate or encourage behind the back of its partners a policy that would be dangerous to peace. No more shifting alliances, but genuine, permantly established communities of nations.

For us there is still another reason behind the policy of European unification. Through the division of our own country we have sensibly experienced what it means for Europe to be divided. And many of us have learned that the solution of the German question is dependent upon what the relationship between the divided parts of Europe becomes. Encouraging the unification of Europe cannot mean that one is satisfied with having the western part of Germany merely incorporated into the western half of Europe. Above and beyond the unification in the western half of Europe, the nations of Eastern and Western Europe must be brought back together again, though in an altered condition and on a new basis. The goal of our European policy thus has a broader scope than just European unity. Beyond this, there exists a legitimate German interest in, and responsibility for the whole of Europe.

The Long Range Goal of Permanent Peace in Europe

The beginning of the European unification policy after 1945 occurred during a period of intensive confrontation between East and West. The unification in the West was understood by many to be a part of the Cold War. Many believed that the main necessity was the containment of Communism. It was because of this that European policy was given an all too narrow, defensive and negative stamp.

The Cold War in its old sense was behind this, but difficult divisions continue to persist. These leave no room for illusions, but they are not to be dealt with through remaining a prisoner of obsolete assumptions. One must have the ability to think beyond the present and to fix the sights upon the tasks of the future.

It is my opinion that the European policy is stronger when it excludes an anti-Soviet bias.

I believe that Europe should not unite against something, but for something, namely for the betterment of the European nations and for their constructive role in the world.

I believe that our European policy must be harmonized with the long-range goal of a permanent peace in Europe.

There must be a change of emphasis. We are already well along the road to effecting this. Not only in the West, but also in the East has the understandable interest in overall European co-operation become clearer.

The significant economic potential of the Common Market could not be long disregarded. Even in the Eastern countries the inherent economic possiblities are not being ignored. Leaving the consideration of the various systems aside, one is confronted with the question of genuine co-operation based on legitimate interests. Such a co-operation could be envisaged as corresponding to the present state of the highly developed nations of Europe, who, in their relationships to each other are first and foremost customers, and only secondarily, competitors. The Eastern European nations cannot escape this law of industrial development either.

Reconciliation and co-operation, as we understand them in our efforts to achieve better relations with the nations of Eastern Europe, have already been attempted and realised in Western Europe. And we know that there can be no permanently successful East-West policy without a solid and forward-looking West to West policy.

Extension of the European Community

The establishment of the European Communities and their development into an important component of international relations are the fruits of a successful Western policy following the Second World War. We can, with some satisfaction, take note of the fact that the Western European states who originally remained aloof from the European Communities, now almost without exception, are making efforts to join them or to form some type of association with them. The EEC has in the last few years made so much progress that no member nation can now afford to opt out of it without harming itself.

The West German Government stands by what it has repeatedly stated in its declarations. This means we are for the extension of the European Common Market, and we are making definite efforts towards this extension.

There are people who believe it represents a weakness and we make this statement without qualification. There are people who accuse us of playing one side against the other. They have neither understood us nor the situation. We are not intending to irritate either Paris or London, but it is our intention to further what we consider necessary without risking what already exists.

Inclusion of Great Britain in the Common Market

The economic reasons for the incorporation of Great Britain, as well as Ireland, Denmark and Norway, whose applications for entry were presented simultaneously, are obvious: a greater distribution of production makes possible more efficient industrial and agricultural output and a better retail supply system. Increased competition strengthens the dynamic forces in an economy.

Great Britain is a market of 55 million consumers, which compares with 180 million in the EEC, and 60 million in the Federal Republic of Germany. The gross national product of Great Britain amounts to more than that of France, but somewhat less than that of West Germany. The entrance of Great Britain would increase production and economic efficiency in the EEC by one third. If the other EFTA countries joined with the EEC, the economic potential of the Community would increase by more than fifty percent. In a score of fields Great Britain can point to significant technological achievements, as for example in Aerospace, aircraft, rocketry, atomic and computer techniques. Bringing this know-how into the Common Market would lead to a rapid increase in productivity, a faster rate of growth and would help to maintain the technological viability of the Common Market in relation to the two super powers. Prime Minister Wilson has recently reiterated interesting proposals for European co-operation in the realm of technology. And I believe that that is an appropriate topic for serious consideration in Brussels.

These advantages, however, must be seen against a background of certain difficulties that are bound to arise during a period of transition, difficulties that in certain areas will come about through more intensive competition. That holds true for example for the European Coal and Steel Community, which in any case is going through a structural crisis, and also for the textile industry. These difficulties would effect important economic interests of the Federal Republic, but we are convinced that here, as well as in other areas, reasonable arrangements for the transition can be found.

The Present Situation Surrounding the Question of Entry

On the question of entry let me first present a brief summary of the present situation:

1. The Government of West Germany shall continue to pursue its European policy. We are convinced that the desire to overcome the existing gaping differences between the EFTA and the EEC and the idea of an economic union for free Europe through the extension of the European Communities will triumph in the end.

2. The discussions that have just begun in Brussels among the "Six" will have to first of all be brought to a conclusion. A final judgement of when Great Britain will be in a position to carry out the stipulations of the Treaty of Rome and the decisions of the Council of Ministers in Brussels in certain important areas can only then be made when direct talks have begun with Great Britain.

3. We have never regarded the entrance of Great Britain, Ireland, Denmark and Norway as a process which could be completed in a short time. The necessary negotiations will take time. But we have believed, and continue to believe, that it is wrong to delay the beginnings of negotiations or to block them.

4. The expansion of the European Communities cannot be separated from a general discussion of the situation in Europe. The Communities can only take on their final form after the solution of this question.

5. We in no way desire to block the continued progress of the European Communities. However, it is anticipated that the tendency to give first considerations to national interests will be strengthened. Unfortunately, it is probable that the European elan which is so necessary for the future solution of outstanding problems will suffer in the process.

6. Whether or not reasonable solutions for transitional difficulties can be found is a question that first must be clarified. The readiness to consider such steps does not alter our conviction that all economic and financial questions, which would be brought about by the entry of Great Britain and the three other nations are solvable.

7. The deep lying reasons which caused Germany, France and England after 1945 to support a policy of European unification — even if not, unfortunately, in harmony with one another — are similar; for all three countries, and this also applies to Italy, suffered a corresponding loss in their own importance, a loss which they sought to compensate for through close co-opera-

tion and association with their European partners. This was not a return to the Big Power politics in the old sense, but it was meant to be a forwardlooking means towards obtaining a peaceful, productive and constructive role in the world.

Great Britain at first attempted to make-up for its lost position as a world power through its special relationship with the United States, a relationship which had long historical and cultural roots. But the shift of the power balance in favour of the super powers has taken much of the significance of Great Britain's relationship to the United States away. Thus there exists today an ever closer relationship between Great Britain and the nations of Continental Europe.

In January 1967, Prime Minister Wilson declared at a press conference that Great Britain, if it should become a member of the EEC, would take part fully in the political discussions of the Community. The identification of British policy with the growing political unity of the Continent would, according to Mr. Wilson, have two important consequences: efforts towards relaxation of tensions between East and West could be better co-ordinated, and an expanded Europe, including Great Britain, would be able to play a bigger role in the world. From the German point of view, one can only welcome such a result.

A serious European policy which would recognize the limits of what is possible to achieve will largely be made by the existing European Communities. These nations are involved in a process of mutual economic integration, which with each further step forward becomes all the more irrevocable. An all encompassing European Economic Union, which out of the various national economies of the member states would forge, for all practical purposes, a unified national economy, is the ultimate goal of these efforts towards integration. Real adjustments in essential areas of the economy however must be made before we arrive at the realization of this goal.

The Necessity of the Atlantic Alliance

We can hardly speak of order in Western Europe and about secure peace without taking into consideration the North Atlantic Treaty Organization. Because of the necessary and desirable participation of the United States and Canada, the alliance extends beyond Europe although its center of attention and main tasks lie in Europe. This defence alliance is and will remain necessary, even taking into account that a changing world continually demands a revaluation of purposes and methods. There is noth-

Whether he was with the President of the African Republic of Malawi, Doctor H. Kamuzu Banda, or with the acting Prime Minister of the Republic of Korea, Park Choong Hoon, (above and below respectively), the Foreign Minister always showed himself to be intimately acquainted with the problems of the developing countries.

ing essentially new in this. That holds true for all alliances, because that is the way life is.

It is well known that a group of nations within the alliance would very much like to see the political consultation and co-ordination within the North Atlantic Treaty Organization strengthened and improved. We would favour such a development, for we have ourselves pointed out that the East-West policy presupposes a certain degree of agreement among the Western partners.

On the other hand, France has rejected the idea of a "common policy" within NATO. But the issue is not concerned with common policy in the real meaning of the word, but rather with the necessity and purposefulness of contemporary forms of consultation and co-operation — this is where opinions seem to differ. In this situation an overbearing insistence on a common policy will not serve the interests of the alliance, but will only sharpen current differences of opinion rather than resolving them.

That cannot be in our interest. We see our task — directly in terms of our European responsibilities — to be that of so dealing with these questions that all involved can eventually reach an agreement. I believe that we can accomplish this, for the differences are neither so large nor so basic as has been occasionally asserted.

A Permanent and Just Peace for All of Europe

All the Allies are, in reality, in agreement that the goal of our policy must be a permanent and just peace for all of Europe. By that I mean a settlement which will allay the causes of tension and division in Europe, which find their most significant example in Germany, and seek to overcome them.

This will be an achievement that will only result after years of unremitting effort. But even now there is much preliminary work that can be accomplished. There should not and will not be anything wanting in our readiness to undertake this work.

Without doubt renunciation of the use of force and threat of force, and declining to interfere in the internal affairs of other states will be those things that will have to be dealt with first, if one is considering the elements of a European settlement.

European security in the future will have to be guaranteed through something more stable than just a balance of terror, something better than the stockpiling of military might in the heart of our continent. These are problems that we are currently considering. We shall have something concrete to say regarding this at the appropriate moment.

In the case of any imaginable general European settlement one will have to proceed on the assumption that the various political, economic and social systems of the participating states will have to be respected. The right of every state to determine its own political, economic and cultural system for itself must be seen as a basic fundamental.

The multilateral and bilateral relations between nations must be in harmony with the principles laid down in the United Nations Charter. It would be good if the rights to freedom of movement and information were more generally carried out in Europe.

A European peace arrangement would have to secure for all states in Europe sufficient lasting stability. It should not exclude, or make more difficult a just and permanent solution to the German question.

It is important first of all to create what has been called an "atmosphere of trust," that is, a climate in which at length the solution of great political problems would be possible.

Many of the East-West relations which in the past few years have arisen at the diplomatic and also non-diplomatic levels could help to create this climate. In spite of this it remains a long, tiring and unspectacular road that we have to travel along. But we have to travel this road even farther than we already have.

Co-operation with Eastern European States

First of all we are concerned with the further development of cultural and economic relations with the Soviet Union and the nations of Eastern and South-Eastern Europe. To the extent that these nations are prepared for various useful forms of co-operation can be foreseen and realized. Encouraging beginnings have already been made in spite of difficulties.

Much could yet be done, and I would like to emphasise this, in the realm of disarmament and security, arms inspections and arms limitation.

The German-Soviet talks on essential aspects of European security cannot of necessity comprise more than Germany's obligations to the Alliance, but they can be of significance to more than the parties directly involved.

The German-Rumanian relations are developing in terms of the expectations that both sides had on the occasion of opening diplomatic relations at the beginning of this year.

With the dispatch of Otto Heipertz, Chief of the newly established Trade Mission, to Prague, relations with Czechoslovakia at the turn of the year will be established in accordance with the agreement worked out in August 1967 by Special Ambassador Bahr. Relations between the Federal Republic of Germany and Yugoslavia hopefully will be promulgated in the form that the present state of relations indicates as probable.

The West German government has repeatedly emphasized that it attaches greater importance to the desire of reconciliation with Poland as an element of European peace arrangement than to any other consideration. Cardinal Döpfner has recently stated that the normalization of German-Polish relations is the great task of the future. I believe that seen from the perspective of history, the reconciliation with Poland will one day have the same degree of importance as the reconciliation between Germany and France. Warsaw's current thinking on this matter is still very much concerned with pre-conditions. We are prepared to negotiate on all agreements that could be achieved under the present conditions.

Acknowledgement of Efforts Made by the Foreign Ministers of Friendly Nations

At this point I would like to thank a number of my Foreign Minister colleagues for having so tactfully supported our efforts in their talks with East European governments, helping to bring our relationships with these countries to more intimate levels of communication. A list of those who have in the last few weeks spoken favourably concerning the Eastern policy of the German government in conversation with Eastern European diplomats in various cities would include, among others, the Danish Foreign Minister Tabor, the Norwegian Foreign Minister Lyng, Swedish Foreign Minister Nilsson and my colleagues from the Benelux countries — Luns, Harmel and Grègoire. In making special mention of their efforts, one cannot forget the preceding consultations carried on by the French, British and Italian Foreign Ministers. We are confident that the explanation of our peace initiative, and our efforts to relax tension, through the representatives of friendly states contributes to winning understanding and acceptance in Eastern European capitals for our sincere efforts.

Strengthening of Scientific and Technical Co-operation

Our economic relations with the Eastern European Nations are not developing at all badly. The economic efficiency of a, hopefully, expanded European Common Market with a subsequent co-ordination of Eastern trade policy will make the Eastern European nations more than ever aware of their real interest in an expanding East-West trade.

In this connection we are also thinking of an exchange of technological knowledge. The Federal Republic of Germany is interested in bilateral, as well as a European-wide, strengthening of scientific, technical and cultural co-operation with the Soviet Union and everyone of its allies. This holds true for Eastern European countries and the other half of Germany, which we wish to exclude neither from the policy of co-operation, nor from the efforts to relax tensions.

The business report of the Friedrich-Ebert-Stiftung points to an increase in scientific exchanges with Eastern European countries in the past year, to seminars that have been sponsored, and to journalists and important figures in the field of adult education that have been invited to West Germany for purposes of study and the gathering of information. I hope that this work will be continued and that students from East European countries can be assisted through the scholarship programme of the Foundation.

It would be worthwhile to include the subject of aid policy to a greater extent in the East-West dialogue. Here also one notes the sign of a growing mutual interest. In any case, an exchange of experiences on this subject would be useful. And our partners from the nations of the Third World must understand how the two components of our European policy — West-West and East-West — can also help them.

Above and beyond all specific topics, we wish to develop a "context of good neighbour relations." However, we wish to build on that a peaceful co-operation which will leave behind the hostility and divisions of the past.

A Responsible German Policy

When one speaks of Germany as being on the boundary of East and West, one has mentioned only a geographical truism. It is also politically a truism that the German question has become the key problem to the security and peace of Europe.

We owe it to our European partners and to ourselves to carry on a German policy in the context of our European policy as responsibly and as realistically as possible. Wishful thinking can never solve a problem. It can only make it worse.

In the other part of Germany there exists and governs a political system which does not meet with our acceptance, but with our rejection; but it does exist and it does govern. We do not want to just maintain a common substance of our nation in the memories of men; and in the last analysis, it is our responsibility for our function in the center of the force-field between East and West, which bears so heavily on peace in Europe, that makes us not want to do it.

Positive Proposals for Lessening the Division in Germany

Here we are not concerned solely with the question of who recognizes or does not recognize whom. Here we are concerned with men and with peace. We have good reasons for not wanting to legitimize the present international situation through international recognition and for not wanting to recognize the other part of Germany as being a foreign country. We have made positive proposals in the belief that one should exclude from discussion that area where no agreement is possible and instead concentrate on those areas of mutual interest where agreement could be possible. I believe that the authorities in East Germany will not be able to escape the recognition of what is expected of Germans in both parts of their nation: namely, that they begin to live peacefully with one another inside their own nation, to associate with one another compatibly, not to burden their people with unnecessary troubles and not to endanger peace in Europe, but to make it more secure.

When the German Republic after 1918 was facing problems affecting its national integrity, the problems were of a different nature compared to those facing us today. Friedrich Ebert said something which has a direct bearing now as it did then: „No one should be forced into the union of a German Republic, but neither should anyone be separated from it by force who wishes to be part of the Republic. We wish to establish the basic right of self-determination as the foundation of our state in both domestic and foreign policy.

If the Germans in both parts of their country had the possibility of working together in the interests of humanity, peace and their material welfare, this would not only have a positive effect on relations with Eastern European countries, but would favourably influence the entire European development.

Understanding and Unity

Whoever would dismiss the efforts towards such a European policy as naive and illusory or would give up the task as hopeless would completely renounce any possible German contribution to a European peace. He would take away from the German people that which it, without presumptuousness, most needs to be made aware of — its historically necessary role between East and West. Whoever does not see that, or denies it, leads our people into political isolation and impotence.

The present status of weapon development in the world makes it clear enough that there is no other way than peace. Our thoughts are only a little ahead of their time. They will prevail even in the East.

We are not alone in our intention to encourage understanding and co-operation. The peoples of Western Europe are with us. They have also drawn a positive conclusion from the horrors of the past. But also in the East there are many who agree with this conclusion which signifies European co-operation, European understanding, European unity.

This insight has already brought about tangible results. Only on the basis of a common, expanding European market can we come to grips with the tasks which science and technology have reserved for us in the coming decades. However the particular forms of co-operation may develop, this is a task which we must discern as extending beyond the momentary division between East and West.

The Way to a Unified Europe

The industrialized nations of Europe are obligated and are in a position to open up the way to the underdeveloped nations to economic and social progress at a faster rate than heretofore. We invite the Eastern European regimes and particularly the government of the Soviet Union, to unite with us in friendly competition towards this goal. Deep unrest in the world, the latent danger of a world wide conflict stemming from the economic chasm existing between north and south places all of us, in both Eastern and Western Europe, in a position of historic responsibility.

Finally, I should like to return once more to that time in history when Friedrich Ebert gave an example of what it means to shape a German policy in terms of European responsibility. The violence which he foresaw was later, through its radical right-wing forerunners, to politically defeat him. His wish to be left alone to wander through the "rustling woods" in the vicinity of Heidelberg was not to be fulfilled. The way to Europe which the leading men in the Weimar Republic had forged for the German people was to be rudely and suddenly blocked in 1933. Ebert was himself to experience physically the way fanaticism and intolerance destroyed ones feeling of responsibility. But at no point did he lose his optimistic faith in his mission.

In 1920 he was in Karlsruhe to visit the art gallery. His close compatriot Hans Thoma appeared at the reception. With pride Thoma pointed to the hall containing his paintings, and said: "Herr Reichspräsident, look at my world; it is as I have seen it."

"Yes, Meister Thoma", replied Ebert, "the art work of the state is not so radiant; this perfection is still found to be lacking in it. However, we are just at the beginning and one day there shall be states like your work — tranquil and peaceful ..."

We are still far from realising this vision — we are experiencing this just now in renewed tensions between Turkey and Greece. But if one does not only wish to lament the present situation, and is not satisfied only with hoping, then one must do something constructive to help establish peace in our part of the world. The European policy which I have here explained is for him.

Building Bridges to Neighbours in Eastern Europe

Contribution to the Yugoslavian magazine "International Politics" on June 1st, 1968.

I.

All political action must proceed from the realities: from facts, not from aspirations. Any policy that ignores this principle runs the risk of being wrecked.

But to acknowledge realities does not mean to accept them as unchangeable or incapable of development and improvement. Few political realities are so good that they deserve to be perpetuated. Progress is only possible when existing forms are called into question. One cannot arrest world history at any given point. Those who make policy must be aware of the past. No responsible politician in Germany can ignore the causes and consequences of the Second World War. We know that we must answer for many things that were done in the name of Germany. This is one reality. Another reality is that half the Germans living now were not yet born in 1933 or were too young to bear any responsibility for the twelve years of Hitler's dictatorship. The young generation cannot accept the burden of this terrible past. The disorders of recent weeks make it clear that restless young people in Germany are reacting, questioning and protesting just as in many other countries of Europe. Our youth speaks German and feels European. For them Naziism is history, not experience. German youth does not share the feelings of a defeated people. They express themselves freely, foolishly, cleverly, unrealistically and progressively about Vietnam, Israel, professors and politicians, just like their contemporaries in Paris, Rome, Prague or Warsaw. These young people could turn to nationalism if people abroad treat them as if they were their own fathers and grandfathers. They might also show nationalistic tendencies if these fathers for some reason fail to represent the interests of the nation adequately. What is regarded abroad as a new right extremist danger does not merely consist of old Nazis, it contains an element of youthful protest against older people who, all too aware of their guilt, have become prisoners of the past. And of course, in Germany as elsewhere, there is a residue of people who have learnt nothing and do not want to learn. It is understandable when such things are observed with particular attention abroad, but those who doubt should know: Bonn is not Weimar. The situation today is not comparable with the situation at that time, neither internally nor externally. The overwhelming majority of Germans condemn radicalism. And we shall know how to prevent any danger arising from German soil ever again.

In past years, the Federal Republic of Germany has provided tangible proofs of its trustworthiness. It has allied itself closely to a number of European countries and has made strong efforts towards West European integration. We have voluntarily given up a part of our national sovereignty. As everyone knows, our armed forces are subject to international command. We are the only state in the world up to now that has renounced the production of nuclear weapons. We have submitted our entire atomic industry to international, i. e. European controls. We would rejoice in the banishing of human fear of atomic conflict by means of an internationally acceptable treaty to ban nuclear weapons. This should further lead to a comprehensive control and limitation of armaments and finally to the destruction of all atomic weapons.

II.

Among European realities is the still profound division of the continent and — apart from neutral states — the apportioning of its parts to two highly armed power blocs. For Germans, this division runs through the middle of their own country. It divides what geographically, historically and culturally belongs together. This state of affairs is unnatural and unreasonable; it has also proved to be dangerous.

The desire for peace, balance and cooperation has strengthened in Europe. The European nations are searching for possibilities to loosen these rigid fronts. They are discovering areas of mutual interest. Even as loyal members of one or the other alliance, they are stressing their national and European identities. Over and above membership of the power blocs, the future is beginning to appear in voluntary cooperation as partners rather than dependents. It can be seen that ideological differences need not stand in the way of objective dialogues and overtures. There are areas of mutual interest between West and East European states and the seeds of pan-European solidarity.

This promising, if still paradoxical process of objectivisation can be encouraged by a consistent policy of relaxation. A return to the methods of the Cold War would destroy any prospects for understanding. It would harden the antitheses between the power blocs, instead of reducing them. This would be bad for the whole world. It would be particularly bad for Europe.

The Federal Republic of Germany has a vital interest in achieving a peaceful balance in Europe. The Germans would inevitably be drawn into any armed conflict between East and West. They would be the first to experience the devastation. Their national existence would be at stake: the accumulation of troops, military equipment and atomic means of destruction in the small area of Germany is unique in the world.

So for this reason, too, our primary aim must be the safeguarding of peace in Europe. All other problems, including that of German partition, are subordinate to this aim.

The keystones of our policy are: reduction of tensions, improvement of relations and preparatory contributions to a European peace settlement. Our geographical position gives us a special responsibility. For centuries, Germany has acted as a bridge between eastern and western Europe. We want to try and rebuild bridges which have been destroyed. This is why we want to work together with our eastern neighbours, who share this ambition, in all fields of economic, cultural and — if possible — political life.

III.

Our relationship with the Soviet Union is of central importance to further development. This results in the first place from a valuation of actual conditions and interests in East Europe. Apart from this, the Soviet Union is one of the Powers which bear a special responsibility for Germany as a whole. It would be absurd and unrealistic to follow a policy directed against the Soviet union. It would be just as illusionary to want to exploit possible differences between Moscow and its allies. Without the cooperation of the Soviet Union, it would be impossible to organize peace in Europe. We are trying to improve our relations with the Soviet Union, which are far from being as good as we would wish. We are attempting to arrange discussions on matters in which a partial understanding may now be possible. This is true of various aspects of bilateral relations. Some headway has been made towards the discussion of difficult questions. We have offered to exchange declarations renouncing violence with the Soviet Union and other members of the Warsaw Pact. Our policy should not be interpreted as consisting only of assurances. On the contrary, we are ready to be taken at our word in concrete discussions and to make our honest contribution, so that the agreed renunciation of violence can become an element in the European peace settlement for which we are striving.

Renunciation of violence means, among other things, to agree with the partner that existing borders will not be altered except with the consent of those concerned. This is true of all borders, so far as the government concerned is prepared to make such agreements with the Federal Government. We have also specifically addressed this offer to the G. D. R., which we do not regard as foreign territory but which we did not want to exclude, in the interests of safeguarding peace, relaxing tension and objective cooperation.

In the case of Poland, renunciation of violence would of course include the border problem. It is very important to us to achieve good relations with Poland. Her need, after the suffering of the past, to live at last within secure frontiers and not to be a "state on wheels" is natural and understood. On our side, we ask understanding for our desire for a peace settlement which does not simply impose burdens on our people but also opens up possibilities.

Renunciation of violence would be a great step towards relaxation in Europe. It would smooth the path to further agreements on European security.

IV.

The overwhelming majority of Germans know that they will only find lasting peace and real tranquillity when they have achieved a settlement and reconciliation with the peoples of East and South-East Europe. The foundations of our policy — as it has been consistently developed over the last year and a half — are, here as elsewhere, respect for independence, equality, the principle of non-intervention and regard for the achievements and societies of others.

We were especially concerned about the clarification of our relations to the Socialist Federative Republic of Yugoslavia. In January this year, our governments reached agreement on the opening of diplomatic relations. This step attracted international attention. In West and East, as well as in the states of the Third World, this normalization was assessed as a constructive contribution to relaxation. It was made possible because neither side insisted on pre-conditions and both governments were led by objective considerations. The result was a success for reason and goodwill.

We know that Yugoslavia enjoys great respect in the world. Her achievements in reconstruction and reform have been highly praised. Her independent position and her pragmatic foreign policy, which serves the interests of peace, have brought her considerable international prestige. One of the main elements in future German-Yugoslavian relations will certainly be economic cooperation. The requirements of both economies are complementary. German industry has found a rewarding export market in Yugoslavia. For Yugoslavia, which in the framework of plans and reforms wishes to speed up economic growth, trade with the Federal Republic of Germany is of great value. Both our governments are currently attempting to even out the balance of payments, as Yugoslavia is burdened with a passive balance. Additional facilitation and support of Yugoslav imports and the possibility of technical, scientific, financial and economic cooperation are being considered. We are hoping for the early conclusion of a long-term agreement on goods and currency exchange.

Exchange in other areas also serves the interests of both countries. The Yugoslavian workers in the Federal Republic are useful to our economy and are at the same time contributing to financial relief in their own country.

Increasing numbers of German holiday-makers are spending their holidays in Yugoslavia. This brings currency to Yugoslavia.

Cultural exchange is another worthwhile task. Here, too, we hope soon to conclude an agreement, which should be as unbureaucratic as possible and smooth the path to free, unhindered exchanges.

We would also be glad if both countries could come a little nearer politically. Questions of security in Europe could provide a suitable area for this. The Yugoslav contribution could be of great importance.

V.

Our concept of sefeguarding freedom and a settlement in Europe does not imply isolation of the other part of Germany. The opposite is true, and I am anxious to stress this once again. One of the realities in our continent is that the government in East Berlin is an important ally of the Soviet Union. We are not unaware that the G. D. R. possesses a considerable economic potential which corresponds to the abilities and industry of its people. But the lasting existence of one German nation, the feeling of belonging together of its people are also realities. The overwhelming majority of our people on both sides of the Elbe want to live together again one day and until then, at least be able to pass through senseless barriers. No one can expect of us that we give constitutional recognition to the partition of Germany. No nation with a comparable fate would behave any differently.

Yet we are conscious that the overcoming of German partition will only be possible after a long and gradual process of relaxation. The German question can only be resolved in a Europe in which East and West have found their way to peaceful cooperation. Until then — so we believe — the two parts of Germany should try to live in a state of settled neighbourliness. The present Federal government has made various proposals as to how Germans in East and West may achieve a modus vivendi, without one side being forced to make intolerable concessions to the other.

Irrespective of the known differences in principle, we have offered to conduct discussions with the government in East Berlin. Any agreement resulting would contribute a great deal to relaxation. We hope that in the long run those responsible in the G. D. R. will not cut themselves off from the mutual interests of the European nations.

VI.

Europe is faced with great tasks. Her economic growth, the raising of her scientific and technical achievements, the exploitation of her human and material resources, the living standard of her population, her political future will all be in doubt if we do not succeed in achieving more generous and extensive cooperation. It is not only in time that we are nearer to the year 2000 than the year 1900. The self-sufficient European nation-state is a thing of the past. Taking the concept of Europe seriously involves the ability to look further than one's own region.

With the European communities in the West, we have started a process which could serve as a model for further and more extensive cooperation. The advantages brought by the coalescence of the Six are overwhelmingly greater than any difficulties of adjustment. Results have far exceeded expectations. Those countries that at first feared competition can point to outstanding successes. There ist every reason to believe that an extension of this process of cooperation would meet with equally gratifying results. It is clear that the present dimensions of the E.E.C. are insufficient to do justice to the needs of future cooperation. Without Great Britain, for example, the problems now facing us in Europe can hardly be solved. Nor would we wish to forego cooperation with the Scandinavian countries and other interested nations. We are striving to create a Europe larger than the E.E.C. We also want a Europe that is larger than Western Europe. Only a Europe working as a whole in peace, security and cooperation can be an effective element of stability. It could make a decisive contribution, beyond Europe, to the safeguarding of peace and to material prosperity in the world.

I believe that a common task awaits the developed nations in Western and Eastern Europe. We all bear responsibility for ensuring that the future of humanity is not endangered by the contrast between sated and starving peoples. We should make mutual efforts to give the "Have-nots" a change of improving their position. It would be senseless to continue squandering our forces in fruitless opposition. We should rather try to harmonize the means at our disposal in the most rational possible way.

Here and in the exploitation of the scientific and technological revolution lie the creative tasks of our time. Here it will be seen whether the European nations can turn their eyes from the past, whether they comprehend the challenge of the future and can show themselves capable of mastering the tasks that lie ahead. It is my hope that we shall come to understand the signs of the times.

The Federal Chancellor

Tolerance and Solidarity
with Fellow Human Beings

Speech to mark the opening of "Brotherhood Week" in Cologne on March 21st, 1971.

The United Nations have proclaimed — and the Federal Republic of Germany has not ignored this — that 1971 should be devoted to the "struggle against racism and racial discrimination." On this March 21st, many countries of the world are remembering that exactly eleven years ago sixty-eight people had to die in Sharpeville, because they demonstrated against Apartheid.

Brotherhood Week this year also has a universal connotation. Moreover, the societies for Christian-Jewish Cooperation have placed their annual work like this function under the subject of "Human Races — Human Rights." We should point out, however, and that to others that there are still and still remain problems which derive from what man calls or regards as "Races." That human rights must be upheld where it is a matter of belief and conviction, of origin and language, of customs and ways of living. To comprehend this there is no need to look at other countries. One does not even need to cross the frontiers of our own state or even our closer homeland.

The cares which exist in this connection cannot be overcome by declamations of good will and by festive speeches. The magic of the words humanity, human rights, human dignity, human love and also brotherhood are threatened with losing their power in the course of political life.

I well understood Heinrich Böll when last year he spoke so angrily about the questionability of gala speeches and ceremonies and their "humanitarian tremolo." People may have objected to this irritated objection. I think Böll forced us to listen more carefully to false interim and ancillary, also in the case of one's own words. And we have also reason to remember that not so very long ago we heard all about the angry formula of "humanitarian spleen." Humanitarianism became lost in this. It became lost in the terrible everyday nature of dying, of murder and being murdered, of disgrace and lack of rights. At that time not only words lost their meaning, but everything they symbolized, too. Prudence is called for here. This is an argument against pathos which satisfies nothing but itself, against good will which becomes exhausted in the gesture — but also an argument against a cynical devaluation of principle, without which human humanity is inconceivable and incapable of existence. — I understand Heinrich Böll's philippic as an examination of our responsibility. Responsibility is rooted in conscience. The perspicacity of consciousness is not a planned aim which could be found in a government statement. But it is the point of departure of all internal reforms which are for me not only a social and state, but also an intellectual programme.

As you today have invited the Federal Chancellor, you must expect that he will deal — inwardly and outwardly — with concrete and also topical questions. Let me begin with the word which the Federal Government said on this day in reply to a question of the Opposition: "The Federal Government understands by internal reforms changes stagewise of our state and social reality, based on those values which determine a free and progressive society in the social and democratic state. We want

— more humanity in our society
— equal chances of life
— more social justice
— more freedom for the individual
— more security within the country and without
— more cooperation of the citizen in our communal life.

A policy which is directed inwardly and calls for reforms is also necessary in order to balance tensions with consideration of the respective resources, so that scientific and technical progress on the one side will arise anew between the individual and social requirements on the other side. Reforms carried out in good time overcome fear of the future and create security in the longterm."

When I quote this, I do not want to pat myself an the back, but I want to say: those who speak of human rights today, they should first of all start with themselves, with their closer environment, in their own countries. I was and I am against he inclination towards escapism, which one encounters time and again among intelligent, younger people. That means: I am against the pointing finger, which — on the basis of a well-founded indication by the former Minister of Justice and Federal President — causes to forget how many fingers are pointed at ourselves. I am against self-justice, which appears all too often and all too easily, if foreign and distant countries examine us critically. "Charity begins at home" — and it also begins at home with human rights.

Africa is far and some of our fellow citizens may think that racial discrimination is no longer a problem for us or at least an abstract one.

It is true and has become abstract in the figures of the millions of victims, where the destiny of the individual became lost. The question of minority at that time — if it was one — was dealt with by expulsion and murder. But the problem remained. As Foreign Minister of the Grand Coalition 1969, I signed on behalf of the Federal Republic of Germany a convention of the United Nations, which commits every state to remove all forms of racial discrimination. Did I find this easy to sign? — In the good feeling that we were justifying that demand? It was not so simple and in the meantime it has not become more simple.

When I was in Warsaw at the beginning of December, the burden of recent German history, the burden of a criminal racial policy lay on me. I did what people do when words fail them and thought on behalf of my fellow countrymen — of the millions of murdered people. But I also thought about the fanaticism and suppression — despite Auschwitz — which had found no end. Those who want to understand me could understand me; and many in Germany and other places have understood what I wanted to say without words. Some used this occasion to make unpleasant commentaries, but I ask: where if not there where the Warsaw Ghetto stood, would be the place for a German Federal Chancellor to trace the burden of responsibility and overcome guilt from this responsibility!

But let us remain at home: I read overwhelming reports about difficulties which coloured students have encountered in their search for a room, or that they were at a disadvantage. I also read that coloured American soldiers in our country come across prejudices which are scarcely different from those of their soldiers in their own country. I know that the integration of a person from an alien sphere of influence in a different kind of society is not easy. It calls for a high degree of reciprocal adaption. It demands tact, consideration and tolerance. But I also know that arrogance and a wrong feeling of superiority are to be met with where people have a high opinion of patriotism. It would be patriotic to meet young people who are sent to us from other continents — whether in uniform or in civilian clothing — with an openmindedness which would do us Germans an honour outside in the world. And would benefit respect for our nation. It would be the most effective publicity for our cause. Tolerance — made in Germany: that would be something which we could be proud of.

Do not let us remain with the colour of the skin. In this country, there are working more than two million people of different language and different nationality. They, too, are a minority, are not residents and have no roots, but are a fluctuating population. That does not make the question easier: they are all the more in danger of being treated as second-class citizens. In the first place, they are regarded as a source of power, which our economy cannot do without. The simple truth should be said in simple words: if the cooperation of the foreign workers should be taken from us overnight, our economy would encounter great difficulties. In every respect they earn our daily bread with us. This simple fact should pass through our minds on the way to work in the morning. It is true they need work and money here in our country, because they have too little at home. They depend on us. But we also upon them, even more: otherwise they would not be here. One should not ascertain too hastily that the foreign workers enjoy by and large the same rights, the same wages and the same social security. Conscious discrimination is in fact by no means the rule. But do we not always hear depressing examples of an unconscious, even undesired discrimination, of examples of degradation, of scorn, of lack of patience, of respect for others, of lack of simple friendliness and preparedness for help? Worse: there are time and again examples of inconsidered utilization, scandalous cases of exaggerated rents, of living circumstances which should make us ashamed.

I say to everyone with whom it is concerned: we should not permit this society to create a kind of rental proletariat for the lower classes. We should not allow the difference of language to become a difference of class: our free and basic order may not become blind in one eye, if the weaker social partner speaks Italian, Serbo-Croat, Spanish, Greek or Turkish. Here, it is simply a concrete question of popular instruction and of adult education. In this case, nothing is so educational as the good examples.

Many require our help: the sick and handicapped, those without homes. The question of minorities is a key question of our civilization. One has the ability to tolerate minorities in their midst under the right of equality of birth, of equality as such and of good neighbourliness, called the permanent certificate of maturity. This maturity was not passed anywhere with "excellent." We should however strive to pass it perhaps with "satisfactory."

There is many a reason to question the reality of our constitution, the practising of basic laws in our German everyday life, before we look around all too critically in the world outside. The Convention of the United Nations, about which it is worth thinking about here, demands of us in the very near future how everything is to be within our own four walls, before we begin sweeping in front of our neighbour's door. We have no patent morals at our disposal which make easy for us judgement about the problems of other people and other countries. We know how very much the free spirit citizenship in America suffers from tensions which are turning into the elements of a new class struggle. We observe the tragedy in Southern Africa, where the way to a balance and free coexistence between the white minority and the black majority appears to be blocked. We also see the oppressive fact that in parts of Africa and Asia coloured minorities suffer from coloured majorities.

But I may add now — referring to us in the Federal Republic of Germany — that we do not need to descend into masochism. Just as the justified call for reforms may not be forgotten, which was done in the way of reconstruction work in the years behind us, we should not overlook the call for human rights which the Federal Republic today doubtless listens to in the countries of the world in which the rights of freedom of man are furthest developped. In our country, nobody may be prejudiced because of his sex, his language, his origin, his belief or his political conviction. Everyone has the right to develop his personality in so far that he does not harm the right of others and does not violate the basic order laid down in the constitution or the law of morals. That is demanded by our constitution.

And that is not only patient paper. The human rights are rooted in our country not only in the constitution. They constitute an essential element of that constitutional reality which has developped in our country in the course of little more than two decades. We can be proud of what has been achieved but we want to realize that the democratic and social Federal state, about which our constitution speaks, remains a permanent task. Others say we must take the constitution increasingly seriously, that this has given us our republic, that we must take seriously the basic laws which are defined in it.

Those who speak of human rights in our country may not omit to mention what threat hangs over them from every form of political extremism. Our people and other peoples have had to make this bitter experience. We are particularly advised to exercise alertness.

As a result of the clear refusal which the elector gave to political radicalism, the firmness of our democratic basic order has been confirmed. Nevertheless, we must combat with the means at our disposal political extremism wherever it may appear. That applies particularly to those who think they have to assert their aims with force and terror. It applies also to alertness in the case of those who think they can obtain their aims with the media of undermining. All parties and social groups, which bear responsibility in our state are obliged to ward off energetically such attempts. Enemies of democracy cannot expect consideration from us, if they hang round themselves the macabre cloak of "resistance" and if they resort to anarchistic theories.

Here, we must pay attention to the fact that unrest and radical criticism which has seized a part of our population and above all youth should not be equated with political extremism. Here it is often a case of erroneous sub-developments of our society of which we are not aware; e. g. that in our democratic state more injustice asserts itself than we would like to be responsible for; that in our socially orientated federal state more unsocial conditions survive than our conscience may allow; and that the individual has little say in our country than should be the case in a society of adult citizens.

We may not overhear the warning signs of a creative dissatisfaction, if we want to prevent this turning into extremism. The nonfulfilment of justified demands of large sections of our society for more humanization of our democracy, for greater social justice, for greater equality of opportunity and stronger coresponsibility can conceal greater dangers than a group of extremists which always exist in every society.

Most of us very likely agree that we can possibly encounter the danger of such a threatening radicalization most effectively by attacking it at the roots; that is we remove the bases which cause these dangers by reforms in good time. To formulate it more clearly: reforms are inevitable so that the necessary changes in our society do not ensue along an undemocratic path. Our economic efficiency, our social security and our political stability depend on the gap between necessity and the reality of reforms being closed in good time.

A democracy must always face the challenge of its institutions and also its basic and inevitable principles being filled with new spirit and new life. There exists no doubt that we have long since reached a point in our Federal Republic where the interests of the individual and of the population as a whole must be fulfilled by adaption, change and further development.

When I as Federal Chancellor speak about human rights and brotherhood, then I first have to think what the state can do. Tolerance can first develop effectively, also as a social force, if it is excercised by as many as possible. It cannot be commanded from above. At the same time those acting politically should give with their behaviour a good example. They should conduct fairly and as down-to-earth as possible the political struggle with all the strenousness it calls for. Political slander and even calumny should be avoided.

The coexistence of minority and majority requires permanent

scrutiny and correction. If there is a rule here, then it is this: practised humanity is worth more than proclamation of demands. What I mean here can be described concretely; the Federal Government has been criticized because the destiny of the Germans in Poland was not fixed in the Warsaw Treaty. The Peoples' Republic of Poland believes after its experiences of two decades between the two world wars that it can say that a German minority does not exist within its frontiers. We had — just like other Federal governments before us — not the slightest chance to move from this position. However, the Polish government has recognized in connection with the treaty that citizens of German nationality are living in their republic. It said it was prepared to allow them exit to the Federal Republic, if they wanted it. They have kept their word. Month after month, countless resettlers climbed out of the trains in Friedland. They are welcomed by their relatives with open arms. However, they certainly do not have an easy time to fit themselves smoothly into our way of life, which is so different from that they are accustomed to. We can also show them what the will to exercise non-discrimination means.

On a small scale, we may repeat here one of the most significant achievements which our people has made during this century: the integration and amalgamation of twelve million refugees and expellees — a process which certainly did not go without resistance, lack of smoothness, without discriminating accommodation and without resentments. All in all it proved successful. The success of this tremendous restratification proves what a careful policy of inner tension bound up with sacrifices is capable of. This good spirit of our people — and I do not shy away from calling it that — which has proved itself within our frontiers and spread to reconciliation with our western neighbours — it is now to become tensionable and effective also in the will of the Federal Government in our relations with our eastern neighbours. Our concrete policy, which has no illusions and serves détente is the real and true policy of this time.

Now, I am coming to several remarks which concern foreign policy. Let me first of all repeat that we do not want to force ourselves to be judges over others. With generalized assessments and global judgements, we neither help others nor ourselves. Although a quarter of century separates us from the Nazi regime, we should rather behave properly than come forward with penetrating arguments. It is also a question of differentiating rather than generalizing. Ultimately we were not pleased that everything which was German was at one time put in one pot.

That does not mean that injustice which happened outside our frontiers may be disregarded. But no persecuted person, no oppressed minority and certainly no suppressed majority has been helped by pathos. And we are concerned with the question as to whether others should be helped in the first place or whether one should help oneself with declamations. Concrete help for our fellowmen is also of value, when I do not talk about it. The Federal Government has in more than one case of late done the right thing to address clearly the immediate addressees without making much of this. That is pragmatism which is established in firm, basic values.

Bismarck once said, it was a cardinal mistake of the Germans that they not only preferred a policy of all or nothing, but beyond that insisted on a definite method. The Chairman of the German Social Democrats is not often in the position where he quotes "the Iron Chancellor," but I think that Bismarck has — perspicaciously as he was as Foreign Minister — pointed to a mistaken attitude the most tragic consequences of which first appeared after his time, but that by comparison with that which happened until 1945 has influenced our time. The expression of foreign policy being the art of the possible remains topical for us — without anyone believing that we would deny freedom and justice here. Or that we would no longer draw a clear line distinguishing between freedom and servitude.

Naturally we have never overlooked the fact that in East and West the political orders are irreconcilable in their basic values. Despair about this is something I no longer need, even if I say it frankly. With the allegation of injustice we have not enough, but in future less injustice must prevail.

A policy of détente has its own dynamism. It is not a sign of paralysis. On the contrary: it presupposes clear selfconsciousness and unmistakable will to assert oneself. Through realization of reality, it first wins freedom of action and movement and thus the power which it needs to make our insecure freedom more secure, to remove conflict material and thus ultimately one day the mine fields, the barbed wire, the Wall. We are attempting that and nothing else in clear agreement with our Allies — an agreement which does not require daily confirmation.

There are counter-forces — who would want to deny that? But we rely on the power of the future. We do not need a cold war to uphold our order. And we do not need to prove that injustice is injustice. I am not using two yardsticks, quite simply because I only have one: that of freedom, that of right. And this in addition, which some of the rhetoricians, so full of themselves, forget: the yardstick of the possible and of common sense. During my long years and in the twelve years before 1945 I have taken stock — and I have given the opportunity for people to take stock of me. In the sphere of my policy, there is no need to take on the office of official prosecutor.

We are entering the years which lie ahead of us in order to humanize the living reality of the Germans and of the Europeans in East and West. Tyranny does not disappear by taking this path but by making it superfluous or at least limit its arbitrariness. Injustice cannot be overcome by conjuration but by creating more right, not lack of freedom but gives a chance to freedom — smaller or larger —. We do not feel presumptious enough to have found the stone of the wise man for the settlement of all open questions. But we have decided after a time of sterile banding of words in favour of a policy of practical action. We have reached the conviction that disbanding tensions in Europe, which also expands the leeway of people is only possible, if one brings down to earth the relations and creates a climate which makes possible cooperation and a balance of interests.

We have no differing principles on principle in the case of breaches against human rights in various parts of the world. On the other hand, it is of course of some importance, whether a partner — e. g. within the Western community of states — has committed itself to regard democratic principles. This was the background, as is well-known, against which — measured against the European Convention on Human Rights — a decision was taken about the membership of Greece to the Council of Europe.

As far as Southern Africa is concerned, the Federal Government supports the principles of the United Nations. We reject every form of racial discrimination. The Federal Republic of Germany has supported the United Nations Security Council's decision taken in 1963 against Apartheid policy. This applies also to the decision of the Security Council of 1961 on Rhodesia. Let me add as different things are sometimes asserted: we do not supply South Africa with weapons. Consignments for Portugal are connected with the condition that these weapons shall not be used in Africa. Let me underline just as clearly what I said as Foreign Minister: politics and trade shall not go hand in hand without necessity. In the autumn of last year I spoke just as openly with the African delegation under President Kaunda as during my talks in Kenya at the beginning of this year.

We support humanitarian actions of the United Nations in favour of people in Southern Africa, e. g. by means of a contribution to the education and instruction fund of the United Nations for refugees from that region. Without interfering in the affairs of others I can say that a policy of racial rapprochement and the removal of racial barriers is most suitable for leading to a real solution of the problems of this region. We shall always support these aims and give backing to all those who advocate a peaceful, evolutionary development. Let me now talk about what is occasionally held against us, this Federal Government, differing from others, no longer stresses the particular, but normal relations with Israel. And some people then add to this that this has something to do with what we call our East European policy.

Now, in connection with the signing of the Moscow Treaty of August 12th, I stressed clearly for everyone that an improvement of our relations with the Soviet Union should not be an impediment to our relations with third states. That applies fully to Israel. The Israeli government does not see matters differently. It has rejected the assumption whereby the Federal Government's East European policy has a prejudical effect on its relations to Israel. Moreover, it has never criticized that we have striven as much as possible for good relations with the Arab states.

On the other hand, the leaders of the Arab states who think objectively also overlook our relations to Israel. There continues in fact the sign of a special feature: the fact that millions of Jews were murdered in Europe cannot be extinguished — and this is all the more horrible for us and those born afterwards, because under the spirit of enlightenment the symbiosis of Jewish and German culture has shown such an astonishing productivity. We have nevertheless tolerated the proof — and must tolerate — that hell on earth is possible. It was reality.

The name, Auschwitz, will remain a nightmare for generations. Illusions are not aloud: the injuries which in those dark, twelve years were done to the soul of the people, to the victims and to the soul of the people of the perpetrators will not heal so quickly. For it was the image of man which was injured, of man, whom we understand as the image of God. This experience — it is the real catastrophe of mankind, more than all wars and their terrors lie upon Jewry, not only in Israel; and it lies on us Germans. No pointing to a youth which is free and unbiassed helps here. Nobody is free from history. Israel is — and the slogans of radical groups do nothing to change this — the grandiose attempt of a people to create a secure homeland for the homeless. It is bitter that the birth of this state demanded the prize of new victims and new suffering. Who would want to keep quiet about that? Who would want to keep quiet about the misery of the Palestine Arabs? But the role of the arrogant world moralists does not apply to us here. We have rather to recognize the change of causality of suffering and injustice at its origin: here in the heart of Europe. The Federal Republic, the more fortunate of the two German states which grew up out the ruins of 1945, assumed responsibility for the survivors. The Reparations Agreement of the time with Israel is one of the achievements of Konrad Adenauer and the Social Democratic opposition of that time, which we regard as foundation stones of our state. The GDR will not be able to note with satisfaction in the longterm that it has refused its part in Germany's overall responsibility with regard to the Jewish victims of the Nazi regime all over the world. It will presumably learn what it missed here.

We think that we are justifying the duty of our people and its special responsibility, if we with all we can do encourage the will to establish a peaceful belance in the field of tension of the Middle East. To say very much more than that would be presumption. We are of course convinced that our determined peace policy in Europe can be a further factor in international Détente. Not only tensions — also détente can be catching. Not only lack of peace but also the desire for peace can be infectious.

Today, Israel is — despite the geographical distance — one of our close neighbours. The economic and technological exchange is becoming more intensive. And it has become more balanced. The cultural relations have become intensified, here and there. People have gained the courage to rediscover the common heritage, to take it up without reserve and to examine the new with sympathy or with attention. Modern tourism, as questionable as it might be at times, if the desire for understanding in the case of the foreigner who wants to import and export is free from prejudice, has a healing function for Germany and Israel. For they are above all young people who get to know each other in this way. Here, it is important that we in Israel not only encounter new realities, but also old truths: in the country of the origin of the great powers of belief. The churches have now at last taken in Jewry with that realism and frankness, indeed with that brotherhood in their religious exchange, which would have spared us the tragedies of this century, if we had been prepared earlier. It may be that Christianity begins to recognize more clearly its own in the fate of Jewry, for it sees itself today at a minority in the world population.

I admit that one must be careful in using the concept "normalization." Respect for others makes us patient and quietly modest. Moreover the sincere ascertainment of mutual interests is also in such a difficult relationship the most solid basis for their balance and their harmonization.

As far as our attitude to the Middle East conflict is, then I can only repeat what I said in an interview with a Yugoslaw news agency on July 8th last year. I quote: "We are of the opinion that — in view of all that is concerned with the latest history of my country — we should not be indifferent to the crisis and that we should not question Israel's right to live. But we are striving to justify the legitimate interest and to improve our relations with the Arab states." We continue to support the resolution of the United Nations Security Council of November 22nd, 1967. And we hope that on the way of negotiations a just and lasting settlement of the conflict can be found. I see to my satisfaction that leading representatives of the Arab world no longer question the right to live of Israel and recognize that it is there a matter of being able to live within secure frontiers. All concerned will have to make their contribution. And a generous settlement of the refugee problem will not have to play the smallest role in it. It requires international promotion, and the Federal Republic of Germany — which has already rendered refugee aid — will not give less than the others.

Ladies and gentlemen,

In my government statement of October 28th, 1969, I said that we Germans must assume the role of a people of good neighbours inwardly and outwardly. I have tried to make clear what I understand by good neighbourlines. It is the daily test of tolerance towards the other, the other of one's own people, the foreign worker, the coloured student, but also towards the neighbour outside our frontiers in West and East, North and South.

Tolerance and solidarity with fellow human beings needs also constant encouragement by means of images and good examples. The societies for Christian-Jewish Cooperation have with their activity set a tangible sign of this. They must receive our gratitude for their patient and persistent work in the service of brotherhood. I hope that that which they have done and are doing will bear rich fruits.

Development Aid Is International Structural Policy

Statement at the 115th session of the German Bundestag on April 28th, 1971 during the debate on Government development policy.

Mr. President, ladies and gentlemen,
First of all, I would like to remind you of the concept for the Second Development Decade as resolved and published by the Federal Government on 11th February. This provides, for the first time, binding principles for all government departments, as well as information on the methods, instruments and procedures of our development policy. Now everyone, both at home and abroad, can read for himself what the Federal Republic of Germany is doing and will do. This concept has been well received abroad — as we know from the reaction of the O.E.C.D., for example. Its reception here at home, such as it was, was also not unfavourable. I read this as a sign that our development policy, in its decisive aspects, will continue to be upheld by this house.

In my government policy statement of 28th October 1969, I laid special emphasis on development policy. There is no going back on this. I also spoke about the organization of development aid. Now, it is no secret that there are difficulties in all countries in absorbing a new task such as development policy into traditional administrative structures. Those who take an interest in such things will know that the United States, the first country to start development aid and the country which has long borne the main burden, is in the process of re-organizing.

Here in the Federal Republic of Germany, Federal Chancellor Erhard tried to organize the tasks and responsibilities in this field at the end of 1964. It became clear that the measures taken were inadequate. So the Chancellor's Enactment of 1964 was supplemented and modified by agreements between the Federal Minister for Economic Cooperation, the Press and Information Office, the Minister of Agriculture and, above all, the Minister of Economics. When I state this, Herr Leisler Kiep — you raised the subject earlier: unfortunately I was unable to hear your comments — I think it should bring the desired and necessary clarity to all those involved, whether in carrying out or in supervising and critically reviewing policy adjustments.

In the Federal Ministry for Economic Cooperation itself, Herr Eppler undertook the work of reorganization in autumn 1970, of which the effects on subordinate departments have recently been adjusted after detailed discussion with those involved. I do not wish to assert that we have worked out the best forms for all time.

But I do maintain that no federal government has produced a better thought-out or more rational concept for development aid, or a more satisfactory organization.

In recent months, the question has occasionally been raised in public of whether our tasks in the field of development aid and our will to push through domestic reforms might be in conflict with each other. I do not think so. We all know that we are not living on some "isle of the blessed." We live on a globe where mutual dependence is increasing, where privation and violence in one spot affect prosperity and security everywhere else. This must be clear, even to those in our country who do not care much about international solidarity.

One of our domestic tasks is a sensible structural policy, so that economic graduations in the Federal Republic do not lead to tensions which may damage the whole. Basically, we face the same problems in the European Economic Community. Development aid can perhaps be seen as a form of international structural policy, in which not only space and distance but also the extent of economic and social differences and the inherent and menacing dangers often defy imagination. This international structural policy is not in conflict with domestic policies: it supplements and reinforces them.

Our nation — let me underline it clearly from this aspect as well — needs partners in the world, politically and economically. There are countries with which this partnership must begin with aid. But it should not and will not end that way. It should be led further to the increased contact of people, the exchange of ideas and goods, of experiences and efforts, in order to serve the mutual interests of both sides. Development policy is thus a part of our total policy, which cannot be neglected by any responsible government.

I am glad that in this debate — irrespective of controversies over details — all parties in this house have once again clarified this principle. Thank you for your attention.

A Decisive Step Towards European Unity

Declaration at the summer conference of the European Economic Community at the Hague on December 1st, 1969.

I.

If all were well in Europe, we would not have met today. If our Community were already able to speak with one voice our main topic would be foreign policy: the question of a European peace order, negotiations with the states of Eastern Europe, and our interests in the light of the Middle East conflict.

Instead, the success or failure of this conference will rightly be read from whether we can steer the craft of the European Community back into navigable waters. Concentrated on our narrower problems we shall not be able to sidestep the necessary decisions if our fellow citizens are to realize again that Europe is more than a mere question of market regulations, and if the young generation is to see that Europe is more than the recollection of a gloomily glorious past.

We are certainly agreed that our Community should not be a new bloc but rather an exemplary unit and a worthy element of a balanced all-European peace structure. It is in this spirit that the Federal Republic of Germany seeks understanding with the East in co-operation and co-ordination with its partners in the West. The link we have formed with each other is meant to be indissoluble and should continually be strengthened. If we want to achieve the harmonization we need we shall have to support each other, that is to say, we must practise solidarity. On behalf of the German Government I declare that we for our part are ready to do so. In this we have the backing of German public opinion.

But, of course, our public also wants to know what consequences our European commitments have for them. Like all others, the German Government must be able to show that the contributions it is called upon to make are meaningful, reasonable and well-defined, and that the path towards unity in Western Europe we have chosen is politically the right one.

We do not regard this conference as a substitute for the established institutions of the Community. Our presence here means routine.

II.

That is why I say very frankly: The German Parliament and public expect me not to return from this conference without concrete arrangements regarding the Community's enlargement.

This question has kept us occupied for years. By virtue of the

Treaty it is one of the cardinal questions of our Community, and nowhere was it written that we should not deal with this subject until after the transitional period. The German attitude on this point has been known for years, and I feel that we must not put this matter off any longer.

First, experience has shown that putting off the question of enlargement threatens to paralyse the Community. Second, it is in the common interest if the Community were enlarged at a time when we are endeavouring to bring East and West more closely together. Third, the Community must grow beyond the Six if it wants to hold its own economically and technologically with the giants and to meet its worldwide responsibilities.

And I do not hesitate to add a fourth argument: Whoever may fear that the economic strength of the Federal Republic of Germany could cause an imbalance within the Community ought to be in favour of the enlargement for this very reason.

At any rate, I want to say that without Britain and the other countries desirous of entry, Europe cannot become what it should and can be.

The talks preceding this conference gave me the impression that we agree in principle on the Community's enlargement: this should not be underestimated. Here I wish to address myself in particular to the French President: if France responds to our clear will to complete and develop the Community with the trust required for enlargement, this would give us reason for satisfaction and appreciation.

We are not only agreed on the principle, we also agree that the applicant countries would have to accept the Treaties, their aims and the regulations jointly adopted since the Community was established.

We are also agreed that any guidelines we may adopt for the Community's future development should be communicated to the candidates for membership. Once they have been translated into formal decisions, they, too, would have to be accepted by the candidates. Such a procedure would make it possible — and this I consider important — to synchronize Community development and accession negotiations in such a way that neither process will hamper the other but that the two will be of optimum benefit for each other.

Thus, preparations of the basis positions for negotiations have reached a stage where it should be possible in the near future to put them in final shape. I therefore suggest to give the applicant countries to understand that we think it possible to start negotiations next spring.

We should decide during the negotiation itself on the applicants requests concerning adaptation and transition, and then present our decisions to our negotiating partners as the positions of the Community.

One frequently speaks only of Britain, but this should not be taken as neglect of the other applicant countries.

III.

Furthermore, Europe's interest makes it imperative that we should not ignore our future relationship with other EFTA members. From my own country's point of view, I am thinking especially of Austria and Switzerland. Sweden, as we all know, has asked a still open question which in the end it can only answer itself — in close contact with the other Scandinavian countries.

The close economic ties between the non-aligned countries and the Community, the free trade practised within EFTA, and not least the political function of these countries within Europe, make it essential to find a comprehensive economic solution which will include these countries. A community which pursues resolutely its economic development and political objectives can also justify vis-à-vis third countries a solution of that kind which is necessary in the interest of Europe as a whole. Meeting special situations with special measures does not change the Community's nature. It will not itself become a preferential area but will remain a community.

The Federal Government feels that the countries in question should make their wishes known in good time and should be informed of the possibilities open to them. I therefore propose a joint round of talks with both those seeking entry and those interested in other forms of co-operation. Such a meeting should be held as soon as possible after the commencement of accession negotiations.

IV.

Though we shall have to deal here largely with other problems, I think it desirable for us to decide on a new attempt regarding co-operation in foreign affairs. This should mean more than merely resuming and continuing the exchange of views within the Western European Union.

Past differences about who should participate in a qualified co-operation in foreign affairs would disappear if we could put the enlargement of the Community and political co-operation into one perspective. We would thus reaffirm the "finalité politique" of the Community also in a larger grouping, without incidentally the areas of economic integration and political co-operation having to be completely identical.

I therefore propose that we instruct the Foreign Ministers to draft an agreement for the gradual development of political co-operation among the members of our Community, and this on the assumption that it will be enlarged.

The important thing at the moment is that we should closely co-ordinate our attitude on the topics for an all-European conference. I hope that our representatives on the NATO Council will, in the next few days, play a major part in achieving a constructive contribution. Nobody should be allowed to doubt that we, after careful preparation and with the participation of our American allies, wish to help find solutions that will lead to greater security with fewer arms and make possible more practical co-operation between East and West.

V.

The growing integration of our six economies has made the overall economic development of our countries increasingly interdependent. Any economic imbalances between them today have a direct impact on the Community's overall development which is felt quite soon. Inflationary trends in one country quickly become a threat to the stability of another and to the equilibrium within the Community. This leads to distortions and restrictions in the exchange of goods and services and in capital transactions; they also jeopardize the common agricultural market. This kind of development can harm the Community as a whole. We can only ward off this danger by moving more rapidly towards a Community of stability and growth.

My Government is willing to proceed along the road to the economic and monetary union, step by step with a sober and realistic approach. Structural differences between our states and divergencies still existing between the economic targets and conduct of each of us are realities which can only be altered by perseverance and joint efforts. This requires a convergent behaviour of the large social groups.

In a first phase, the harmonization of the targets will have to go hand in hand with effective coordination of short-term economic policy. In this connexion it is important to determine quantitative medium-term targets of economic policy. If we thus succeed in formulating a common economic policy we can implement the economic and monetary union in a second phase.

Such a development will make it necessary to create a European Reserve Fund. Here, too, I offer my Government's full co-operation. Once the essential conditions exist, we shall participate in the creation of the European Reserve Fund and in defining its modalities. We shall then be prepared to transfer a given proportion of our currency reserve into it for joint administration with the reserves proportionately deposited by our partners.

In the past the Federal Government has given proof of its willingness to practise solidarity in monetary affairs. We are in favour of the relevant decisions of the Council being given concrete form, if possible, before the end of this month.

We should moreover try to fix a time-table for the establishment of the economic and monetary union in the sense of an outward-looking stability-minded community. I suggest that the Council take up this important question and be asked to work out the details of such a phased plan in close co-operation with the Commission, and to adopt it some time in 1970.

If we so decide, we shall be giving a clear indication of our solidarity. Let us resolutely start anew.

VI.

We hawe all come to realize the need for the co-operation of our countries in the fields of science and technology; much has been said and written about it. However, we have been slow to act accordingly. Some sensible proposals are before the Community. They must however be imbedded in a coherent European technology policy. This calls for political decisions.

This applies in particular to EURATOM. I say quite openly that it would be unacceptable and alien to the spirit of our co-operation if, while discussing the question of completion, development and enlargement, we were at the same time to allow the future of the EURATOM Research Centre, which was established at great expense, to be placed in jeopardy simply for want of agreement on the provision and use of the necessary funds, which after all are negligible when seen as part of overall projected Community expenditure.

It seems to me that we shall not make progress fast enough using the present method of drawing up very detailed Community programmes which are confined to the nuclear sector and have to be unanimously adopted. We cannot here go into the details of the research programme. But we can, and this I would suggest, show that we all have the will to settle the EURATOM crisis. In order to do this we should agree to guarantee the continued existence of the Research Centre, to extend its activities to non-nuclear fields, and to introduce greater flexibility into its structure and methods of work.

VII.

Whilst I am on the subject of the Community's development I must also say something about its institutions. We are dependent on their functioning in accordance with the Treaty. This will be seen even more clearly when we enter the phase of enlargement.

I suggest that the Council's methods of work be streamlined, the Commission's executive functions widened where the subject matter requires, and the powers of the European Parliament extended, especially to include budgetary control.

The structure of the Community must be brought into harmony with the principles of parliamentary control. In this connection we should also not lose sight of the principle of direct election laid down in the Treaty.

VIII.

Under the provisions of the Treaty, the Community enters its definitive phase on 1 January, 1970. Our Governments have agreed in the Council to start from the assumption that the transitional period will not be extended. Consequently, we shall have to do all we can to bring about the necessary decisions.

It has become apparent from our deliberations in the Council that it will not be possible to finish by the end of the year everything scheduled for completion in the transitional period. This includes matters of special interest to Germany, such as certain measures concerning tax harmonization, trade policy, and in connexion with the removal of remaining internal market restrictions. We trust in the readiness expressed by all members to try and solve the outstanding problems as quickly as possible, and we do not insist on complete solutions by the end of the year.

As we all know, the real difficulties lie in the field of agricultural financing. To the Federal Government this complex problem has both fundamental and practical espects.

We subscribe to the principle of European solidarity which must also apply in the course of the development and enlargement of our Community. The nature and extent of financing are determined by the shaping of agricultural policy. This policy, however, does not work satisfactorily for two reasons:

First, the Community keeps on producing bigger and bigger surpluses. Financing them eats up more and more funds that are needed elsewhere. This is being criticized as uneconomical and is bound to discredit the Community in the eyes of the public, all the more so as the consumers feel that they are being pushed aside. Moreover, if this trend continues, it will exceed our financial capacity. On top of this, our surpluses are a strain on world agricultural markets, and this we must avoid for the sake of world trade. On economic and financial, but also political grounds, therefore, we shall have to make vigorous efforts to master the surplus problem. This certainly calls for fundamental reform of the instruments of agricultural policy, that is to say, the market regulations.

Second, agricultural policy does not function properly because each country has its own unsolved structural problems in this field. These require urgent solutions if we want to balance our overall economic structures. This in turn is the precondition for the necessary economic harmonization at Community level.

The reform of our agricultural structures will have to remain largely the responsibility of our individual governments. In fact, experience has shown that even governments already find it necessary to delegate responsibility for structural policy matters to lower levels. It is imperative that we all press on resolutely with our structural policy and co-ordinate it in such a way that it will meet the requirements of our economic integration.

In order to make sure that there will be no misunderstandings during the discussions in the weeks ahead, must say quite frankly that not only do I have to protect the interests of the German taxpayer but also the future of the German farmer. My programme of domestic reforms includes the development of a modern and competitive agricultural community.

This is the framework in which we see the problem. As a result, the Federal Government will only be able to agree to financing arrangements in the definitive phase if it can be sure that discussions of the surplus problem, that is to say, the reform of agricultural market regulations, are started immediately and continued energetically on the basis of promising concepts. All member Governments will have to instruct their representatives on the Council, together with the Commission, to speed up vigorously the work involved. In this connexion the twofold function hitherto exercised by prices cannot remain taboo. What we need is to elaborate concrete methods in good time enabling us to make an early assessment of the commitments we should have to assume. Only then could the Federal Government recommend to the legislative bodies that they approve the financing arrangements. Such approval is required under Regulation 25/62 which expressly provides for the initiation of the procedure according to Article 201 of the EEC-Treaty.

The German Parliament of course also sees an innate link between agricultural financing and enlargement. Under this aspect I have noted with satisfaction opinions expressed by other governments that the agricultural system, including its financing, will have to remain adjustable, especially in view of the Community's enlargement.

If we can reach agreement along these lines, the way will be open for a definitive arrangement in the field of agricultural financing. The Commission has made proposals for such a settlement to the Council, which, taken as a whole, have their special importance. But it is no mystery to any of us that in the weeks and months ahead we shall have extremely difficult decisions to take on individual points.

IX.

To this outline of my Government's attitude I would only like to add that our choice is between a courageous step forward and a dangerous crisis. What I say here is no different to what I say at home: the nations of Europe are waiting for and urging our statesmen to place the will for success side by side with the logic of history. Europe needs our success.

Let me call your attention once more to the young generation and inform you that the Federal Government wishes a European Youth Organization to be set up. We feel encouraged in this desire by the very good experience we have had with the Franco-German Youth Organization.

Within the orbit of world affairs, our Community, whilst becoming stronger and larger, should pursue a twofold aim: By pooling its resources it should enable Europe to hold its own economically, scientifically and technologically with the super powers and thereby preserve its identity. It should at the same time enable Europe to make a vigorous contribution towards the great task which faces the industrial countries with ever growing urgency: development aid.

We can render our ideals of peace and humanity no better service.

Peace Policy of the European Community

Statement to the Bundestag in Bonn on June 24th, 1971.

Mr. President, ladies and gentlemen,
In my Government policy statement on October 28th, 1969, I said, with regard to the approaching Hague Summit Conference:
The peoples of Europe expect and insist that statesmen match the logic of history with the will to success. This has happened in one important field. In the last round of Luxemburg negotiations, the six member states of the Community and Great Britain reached agreement early yesterday on its enlargement. This means that the European ideal has won a decisive victory. All the governments concerned and the Commission have made construtive contributions towards this result.
Let me now before this house, as I did after the Hague Conference, pay especial respect to the statesmanlike vision of the French president, Georges Pompidou, without whose crucial contribution success would not have been possible.
The same must be said of Prime Minister Edward Heath. His government adhered to the decision of its predecessor and pursued it with determination. It provided proof that Great Britain wishes to join the Community, with its political aims and options, without reservations. This cleared the way of considerable difficulties. In the long run, success depends on the clear political will of all politicians concerned to continue working for integration in the way in which, despite all setbacks, the European Community has begun so successfully. For our own part, I want to express at this time and before you all the thanks of the Federal Government to Federal Minister Walter Scheel and his colleagues for the perseverance, negotiating skill and wealth of ideas with which they have contributed to this success.
The success of these negotiations for enlargement of the Community provide proof of its strength: it will now grow beyond the geographical limits imposed by political circumstances at the time of its founding. Had the Community not produced this strength, hard and justified criticism could not have been avoided. Now, however, the revolutionary proposal worked out in May 1950 by Robert Schuman and Jean Monnet is shown to have been the first and strategically decisive step towards the result of these negotiations. While I mention these two names in an hour which may, without exaggeration, be called an historic hour, let me also remember former Federal Chancellor Konrad Adenauer and the Italian Prime Minister, de Gasperi, who both gave great support

to the start of West European integration. Here, too, let us name one member of this house for his pioneer work in the European Community. I mean Professor Walter Hallstein, the first President of the Commission, who held the post for many years.

Ladies and gentlemen, in December 1969 in the Hague I made clear our opinion that the future of the Community was also and specifically dependent on whether it could master the question of enlargement. In all the intervening months, we have never left any doubt that entry could only be sought and achieved if solidarity between the six member states were preserved. In the course of the negotiations, which have by no means always been easy, it has been possible in diverse contacts with our partners, including personal contacts, to find ways and means of assisting progress in the actual entry negotiations.

What has now been achieved will encourage the further development of the Community into an economic and currency union. The Federal Government will do everything in its power to bring the approaching negotiations on the entry of Denmark, Norway and Ireland to an equally satisfactory conclusion by the end of the year.

At the same time, we shall make every attempt to see that the special relationship with those members of E. F. T. A. who have not applied for entry is regulated, so that these treaties can into effect simultaneously with the entry of the Four.

The Federal Government, ladies and gentlemen, is convinced that the enlarged and, we are certain, internally strengthened Community must keep an open door to the rest of the world economically and will show itself to be conscious of its international responsibilities.

There is no doubt that an enlarged and intensified Community will have its influence on the world political scene. Some observers abroad have perhaps recognized more clearly than we ourselves and others in Western Europe, the potential importance of this Community in international events.

The European Community will pursue a policy of peace — indeed, how could the peoples of Europe do anything else in view of their historical experiences?

In the time to come, it will be the task of the European Community, not to neglect the Atlantic Alliance and partnership with the United States, but at the same time to show itself to be a dependable partner to its East European neighbour states, wherever this may be possible.

Ladies and gentlemen, I believe that everyone in Germany has reason to be satisfied with this important step forward.

The establishment of peace in Europe and the further development of good relations with France are the cornerstones of Brandt's European policy. President Pompidou of France (above) with the President of West Germany, Doctor Heinemann, and Chancellor Brandt at one of his visits for consultations in Bonn. Below, the President of the Action Committee of a United States of Europe, Jean Monnet, in conference in the Federal German Chancellory.

State Visit of Indonesian President Suharto and his wife to West Germany in 1970.

West German Chancellor Willy Brandt took a holiday in Kenya during the month of December 1970. Our picture shows him at a press conference in the Mount Kenya Safari Club with the Kenyan Foreign Minister Mungai.

European Partnership and the Unions

Introductory speech before the Annual Assembly of the European Alliance of Free Unions on October 14th, 1970 in Bonn.

Ladies and gentlemen, as Federal Chancellor and on behalf of the Federal Government I extend a cordial welcome to you, the representatives of a Confederation, which assumes particular importance through its active support for the cause of democratic and social progress in Europe.

We have not forgotten that the free trade unions in neighbouring Western countries — and of course in America — were among the first to hold out a hand to the citizens of defeated Germany after the war. Their conciliatory attitude and their readiness for co-operation were instrumental in easing the way for the integration of the Federal Republic in the family of free nations and helped to make us what we are today, an equal partner in the work of building one united Europe.

The trade unions have a major role to play in the process of European unification. Close co-operation among them is a guarantee that with growing economic integration the interests of broad sections of the population will be preserved. The foundation of the European Confederation of free trade unions last year was an important step along this road.

Unification in this part of Europe is a vital interest of our people. We therefore feel gratified at the fact that the process of European integration is in motion again after a period of stagnation. Much has been achieved in the months that have passed since the Summit Conference in the Hague. The complex problem of financial arrangements within the European Community has been solved and the European Parliament has been given wider powers. Negotiations with the applicant countries have been opened. In addition, progress is being made toward political co-operation. Last, not least, in the social sphere an important step forward has been taken by transforming the European Social Fund into an instrument of European employment policy.

While we can point to some accomplishments, a great deal still remains to be done. The great task of this decade is to set up a European economic and monetary union. We hope that the phased plan drawn up for this purpose can be put into effect as soon as possible. The European partners realize that this new phase of co-operation will require further competences to be transferred. This demands progress also towards the further democratization of the Community.

As for the enlargement of the Community, the Federal Government will do its best to ensure that the current negotiations, which up to now have not been unfavourable, will be brought to a satisfactory conclusion as soon as possible. The accession of countries like Britain, Ireland, Denmark and Norway will strengthen the European Community, both economically and politically.

Another major objective in the near future will be the implementation of an industrial policy that will meet the requirements of a vast economic entity. This calls for urgent decisions regarding European Company Law, the merger of national companies but also control over such mergers, and not least the question of co-determination.

It is understandable that, on the European level, trade unions should devote special attention to this latter question. I am sure there is general agreement that any arrangements in this respect on a European scale should not be allowed to hamper the efforts being made in individual member countries to extend social rights. On the other hand, we should ensure that developments in this direction in the partner states do not impede or delay a European solution.

Our efforts to create a united Europe will remain patchwork if we cannot achieve conciliation with our neighbours in Eastern Europe. The Federal Republic and its partners are agreed that this is only possible on the basis of close Western co-operation. On a previous occasion I emphasized that understanding with the East is the least suitable of all fields for any country "to go it alone," whether in an economic or a political context. This I wish to emphasize most strongly.

We hope that a concerted policy of détente will diminish the present confrontation in Europe, promote economic exchanges, improve political relations, and facilitate human contacts. This task is incumbent not only on governments but on all groups that carry responsibility in our countries. We must all work for the creation of a state of peace in Europe in which our nations will be able to work together for their mutual benefit. Here, too, the free trade unions have an important role to play.

"Obligation to Peace"

Declaration on the 25th anniversary of the end of World War II on May 8th, 1970.

Mr. President, ladies and gentlemen,

Twenty-five years have now passed since the all-out war of the Nazi regime ended in total defeat. After almost six years of war, the guns of Europe were silent at last.

The war begun by Hitler claimed the lives of millions of men, women and children, including prisoners and soldiers of many nations. We venerate the memory of them all. The grief brought by their death and the suffering caused by the war are an admonition to us not to forget the lessons of the past and to look upon the safeguarding of the peace as the final goal of our policies and action.

These days are making us especially mindful of our commitment to peace. We share with other nations the concern about the intensification and expansion of the hostilities in Southeast Asia and the crisis in the Middle East. The Government hopes that the efforts being made on behalf of a peaceful solution to these grievous and dangerous conflicts will soon be successful.

We Germans are thankful that since 1945 we have been spared the scourge of war. At that time, not only did the unconditional capitulation coincide with the collapse o the Third Reich, the existence of the nation itself was in question: The country was occupied; a vast number of our countrymen were without house and homeland; families were scattered, cities destroyed. Hopelessness threatened to stifle the courage to live. To many the possibility of reconstruction seemed doubtful.

The main burden in those years was borne by the women — the mothers. They had already had to survive the anguish of the nights of bombings. Now, rigorous work and the struggle with famine was inflicted upon them. Added to this was the anxiety about their husbands, sons, families. It is fitting to remember especially the women's share in the fate of the entire nation.

The churches and other institutions have already commented publicly on this occasion. The Government's purpose in making a special declaration before the Bundestag today is to recognize that which was. A nation must be willing to look dispassionately at its own history.

For only those who remember the realities of yesterday will be able to perceive the realities of today and to envision the possibilities of tomorrow.

This applies especially to the younger generation. It was not involved in what ended then. The 20-year-olds of today were not yet born. The 30-year-olds were children. And even the 40-year-olds had no part in what descended upon us in 1933. Even so, no one is free from the history he has inherited.

This is brought home to everyone who — as I did just a few weeks ago — stands in front of a memorial at one of the concentration camp sites. This, too, must be seen: what in those days — 25 years ago — was felt by countless Germans as national as well as personal affliction was, for other peoples, liberation from foreign rule, from terrorism and fear. And for the majority of the German people as well, there emerged the chance of beginning again, of creating a constitutional and democratic way of life.

For everyone living at the time, 1945 represented a deep divide. It was also a divide in the history of our people. The map of Europe was drastically altered. Large areas of Germany were joined to other countries. The most conspicuous of the lines of occupation drawn in those times is still the boundary dividing Germany.

In the present-day course of political events, we have still to deal with the political realities that evolved out of the Hitler regime. This is true not only for us, nor for this part of the world alone. World War II ended first in Europe and then—and not until then — in Asia. Its aftermath left other countries divided as well. Bloody conflicts followed. And the first atomic bombs, bringing an end in 1945 to the war with Japan, ushered in the nuclear age with its dimensions of terror — and of progress as well.

in 1945 the United Nations was founded. Its inadequacies notwithstanding, it introduced an epoch of international cooperation — cooperation of an intensity previously unknown. The emergence of a great number of new states, coming at the end of the age of colonialism, contributed decisively at this point. This international cooperation must be broadened so that international tensions can be broken down.

Hence, the Western governments are making efforts to intensify the programme in Europe of peaceful cooperation with the Eastern states. This is being pursued in the realization that peaceful, active coexistence is best furthered when nations join together in approaching mutual problems.

As far as it can, the Federal Republic of Germany is fully sharing in these endeavours. It has become a respected and frequently sought-after member of the world community. This can be a source of satisfaction to us. But we must not forget that the scars left by the war have not yet healed everywhere, that the mistrust towards us has not yet vanished. There are occasions, including minor ones, when it re-emerges.

This, too, is one of the realities that German policy will have to cope with. We can only do so by keeping our policy focussed on peace. In the Government policy statement of October 28, I announced that we would follow up the initiative of our President and coordinate research in the area of peace studies. Since then we have progressed to the point of being able to send out invitations to the founding of a "German Society for the Promotion of Research on Peace and Conflict."

Both Government-affiliated and non-Government-affiliated organizations and agencies — while maintaining autonomy in research — plan to cooperate closely with the society. In his inaugural address President Heinemann spoke of the existence of "difficult fatherlands" and added that one of these was Germany. There was hardly a time when Germany was a more difficult fatherland than in 1945. This was more generally realized then than it is today. Since that time the fatherland concept has become alien to many young people. But regardless of whether we speak of fatherland, homeland or nation, the awareness that Germany exists and that the Germans regard themselves as one people, has not been extinguished.

In 1945 the German people went doggedly to work, and they worked hard — in both parts of Germany. The visible ruins of the war were cleared away. The cities and villages were rebuilt. New jobs were created. Industry and trade flourished in a way that elicited the admiration if the world. In the fields of science, art and culture Germany's isolation was overcome and important new ground was broken.

All this would not have been possible without the participation of those who were expelled from or who fled from their old homes. They coped with their exigencies courageously and tenaciously. They became citizens of the new homeland we shared and a permanent part of our society. This integration may well be regarded as the greatest achievement in Germany's postwar history. And thus, whatever may be asserted here and beyond our borders, an important precaution against the jeopardizing of the peace and for the preservation of freedom and justice has been established. The reconstruction of Germany was the result of the work of people from all strata of our nation. Only the person who can remember what things looked like in 1945 can appreciate the distance covered between then and now. He will also correctly assess the concerns and problems we must wrestle with. He will exercise patience where it is patently clear that solutions cannot be found overnight. But he will be impatient when it comes to helping people whose lives and fortunes are still affected, directly or indirectly, by the war and its aftermath.

We think here of the severely disabled, the war widows and their children, as well as the refugees and expellees who have not yet been able to find a real home. We think, too, of Germans who want to come to Germany but who have so far received no exit permit. And we call to mind that there is a great deal of variation in the assessing of guilt, that there are still prisoners in foreign custody.

In speaking of reconstruction, we do not want to forget the work that has been done in the other part of Germany. Under greater difficulties than ours and under socio-political conditions that they did not choose our countrymen in the GDR (East Germany) have scored successes of which they can be proud and to which we must pay full tribute. Relations between the states in Germany on terms of equality should be based — not least of all — on respect for this achievement. In the years following 1945 we in the Federal Republic of Germany were able to work out a new democratic constitution. Certainly it still requires constant reforms, improvements and amendments. On the whole, however, it is the most liberal constitution — both in precept and practice — in German history. It is due to the strength of our new democracy that — unlike the period following World War I — all parties represented in this house stand firmly on the foundation of the constitution. The most recent Bundestag elections confirmed our ability to turn back enemies of democracy by means of education and persuasion.

The realization of shared experiences and a shared loyalty to the constitution should also make it possible for us to recognize and bear in mind during the airing of political differences the limits beyond which the existence of our democracy will be threatened. The Weimar Republic foundered because political parties did not adhere to these limits. This can be no more allowed to recur than a relapse into nationalistic aberrations.

Effort towards international peace and internal peace belong together. Both mean nothing other than smooth integration. The internal political system of our Federal Republic knows no dominating majority and no anti-democratic minority of any consequence. It is supported by the consent of the people, who express their confidence in the democratic parties from election to election. This democratic system is the guarantee of our freedom.

I call here upon the younger generation to hold to this unswervingly. All young people are free from the dreadful experiences of their parents, but they are also without the lessons — some of them oppressive, some of them imperative — that we were able to draw from them. It would be perilous for democracy if a large number of younger people were to throw the painful lessons of history to the winds and to seek their salvation in radicalism. Such radicalism could jeopardize the reconciliation — partially concluded, partially prospective — with our neighbours.

It accorded with the international political situation as it evolved after World War II that we were first able to come to a rapprochement with the Western nations. This policy was substantially formed by Chancellor Adenauer under our first President, Theodor Heuss.

This was a historic achievement, one that remains the fundament of our policies and the guarantee of our security.

But the division of the world into two great power blocs also split Europe, our country and its traditional capital, into two parts and delayed rapprochement with the Eastern nations. This rapprochement and reconciliation is, as we all know, expecially difficult. But the interests of peace make it just as imperative as an understanding with the West. Apparently we must begin here at the same place where we were in relationship to the West in 1945 or 1949. But it is no longer 1945; it is 1970. In the past 25 years things have happened that cannot simply be annulled. We must recognize then as facts if we wish to make progress.

We face bitter and painful realities, such as the borderline dividing Germany. But there are also hopeful realities, such as the living and enduring reality of one German nation, the firm ties between the Federal Republic and West Berlin and, of no less importance, there is the unmistakeable reality of Europe, which is rich with possibilities for the future.

The two world wars of our century had their origin in the rivalry between the European powers.

From the day of its inception, the Federal Republic of Germany committed itself to and declared itself for close co-operation in Europe. It has held to French Foreign Minister Schuman's declaration of May 9, 1950 — 20 years ago tomorrow. It will continue to pursue this policy and to do everything it can to see that the consolidation of the European states will be one of increasing depth and, where possible, of breadth — initially by means of integration in the West and then, it is to be hoped, through growing co-operation between West and East.

The European consolidation that has begun is probably the one result of the tragic events of 1945 that promises to be most fruitful for the future. It is also one of the most important prerequisites for a European peace arrangement — which must perforce be the goal of the policy of all European nations, Western and Eastern. It may be misunderstood, but I hope that I shall be rightly understood when I say that only a European peace arrangement will be able to draw the line of history underneath that which, for us Germans, is connected with the year 1945.

Serious Start on Settlement with the East

Statement before flight to Moscow on August 11th, 1970 to sign the German-Soviet Treaty.

This is not a moment for big words. Sober judgement and a political sense of proportion are what are needed now.

What is involved in this journey? With the signing of this treaty between the Federal Republic of Germany and the U.S.S.R., a serious start is being made on the long-needed effort to reach a settlement with the East. Our signature will set the seal on the material and personal achievements of Foreign Minister Scheel and his delegation after tough negotiations in Moscow.

With this treaty, the Federal Government fulfils a task which it set itself in the government policy statement of October last year and in the Cabinet decisions of 7th June and 23rd July.

Everyone must know that the Treaty upholds our national interests, that it is intended to secure peace in Europe and that it will serve as a good basis for the development of our future relations with the Soviet Union, but also with other East European partners.

The signing of the Treaty will not bring it into force. The Federal Government is proceeding on the assumption that the signing will be helpful towards a satisfactory settlement of the Berlin question by the Four Powers.

Foreign Minister Scheel and I are flying to Moscow in the certainty that our countrymen understand what is at stake and that our allies are firmly supporting us. In spite of differences in our social systems, this treaty for the relaxation of tension should help to improve the relationship between East and West.

Peace with all the Peoples of Eastern Europe

Remarks made on Moscow television on August 12th, 1970.

My fellow-citizens,
The signing of the treaty between the Soviet Union and the Federal Republic of Germany is an important moment in our postwar history. Twenty-five years after the capitulation of the German Reich that was destroyed by Hitler, and fifteen years after Konrad Adenauer, here in Moscow, had agreed the establishment of diplomatic relations, it is now time to reconstitute our relationship with the East, and what is more on the basis of the unconditional, reciprocal renunciation of force and taking as a starting-point the existing political situation in Europe.

With the work on this treaty, the Federal Government has fulfilled a task it set itself in its policy declaration, in which it says: "Our national interest does not permit us to stand between East and West. Our country needs cooperation and coordination with the West and understanding with the East. The German people needs peace in the full sense of that word also with the peoples of the Soviet Union and all peoples of the European East."

This was and is our guideline, and the treaty serves this work of peace.

I know I am free from wishful thinking, as most of you are. This century, marked by blood and tears and hard work, has taught us to exercise common sense. This common sense has to stand the test particularly when we are witnesses and partners in historical changes. Nor must we abandon it even when we have occasion for satisfaction and fresh hope, when we — I do not hesitate to use the word — can rightly speak of a success.

And this treaty with the Soviet Union is a success of German postwar policy. It is a decisive step towards improving our relations with the Soviet Union and our Eastern neighbours — a quarter of a century after the catastrophe that claimed untold victims from the nations, in the East more than in the West.

It accords with the interests of the entire German people to improve relations with the Soviet Union in particular. Not only is she one of the major World Powers; she also shares in the special responsibility for Germany as a whole and Berlin.

Tomorrow it will be nine years since the Wall was built. Today we have — I confidently hope — made a start in order to counteract the rift, in order that people will no longer have to die in barbed wire, until the day comes when — so we hope — the division of our people can be overcome.

Europe ends neither at the Elbe nor at the eastern frontier of Poland. Russia is inextricably involved in the history of Europe, not only as en enemy and menace, but also as a partner — historically, politically, culturally and economically. Only if we in Western Europe focus our attention upon this partnership, and only if the peoples of Eastern Europe see this as well, can we arrive at a settlement of interests.

My fellow-citizens: Nothing is lost with this treaty that was not gambled away long ago. We have the courage to turn over a new page of history. This should benefit above all the younger generation, which has grown up in peace and without sharing the responsibility for the past, but which must nevertheless share in bearing the consequences of the war, since no one can run away from the history of his people.

The firm embedding of the Federal Republic and her free society in the Western Alliance is in no way vitiated by this treaty. The reliable partnership with America is preserved, just as is the reconciliation with France. Also remaining is the determination to join more and more European States ever more closely together, with the goal of a political community.

The treaty jeopardizes nothing and no one. It is to be instrumental in opening up the way forward. And if it does that, then it will serve peace, Europe and us all.

A New Basis

Statement to the press in Moscow on August 13th, 1970.

We — Herr Scheel, myself and our colleagues — yesterday had over three hours of talks with Prime Minister Kossygin. The conversation was continued at the dinner-table and thereafter. This afternoon we wound up the talks in an hour and a half, in an atmosphere which I would describe as "relaxed."
Yesterday I also had a four-hour discussion with Mr. Breshnev. But in spite of the length of discussion, we were not able to cover all the material. We would have liked to have talked for another four or five hours in order to complete a first general survey. For me — and perhaps also for my partner — the discussion was very illuminating.
I would like to undertake the political evaluation of these talks in Bonn. Quite frankly, I must first put my notes and impressions of the talks in order, during the flight and afterwards. There is sometimes no harm in further reflection.

The communiqué is certainly known to you already. The political interest here was obvious. It was expressed, for one thing, in the fact that the political leaders of the Soviet Union present in Moscow at this time attended the signing of the Treaty. In our talks, foreign reaction to the conclusion of this Treaty was frequently mentioned and appraised. About reaction abroad, let me say this: I'm a bit afraid of the superlatives to be heard here and there. When I hear the phrase "historical importance," I can only say, as a practised Berliner: "Haven't you got it a size smaller?" The fact that this Treaty may be a new basis is really enough for us and for others.
At no point in these talks — and this is in fact a bit of political evaluation — did we encounter even a hint of an idea that we may only have met together to play others off against each other or that one or other of us might part from those with whom we cooperate. Without asking, I was assured by a highly responsible source: we have considered this very thoroughly. We do not want the improvement in our relations to be paid for by a deterioration in your relations with others.
This would have been impossible in any case, but it is important to have it established on both sides.
We discussed practical questions, which will be the subject of further talks. Ministers Schiller and Leussink will be in Moscow next month to discuss practical problems and we shall then sum up

the results at home. This is one consequence of the supplementary talks conducted here by the Foreign Minister.

Let me make the following observation: both partners have established a connection between this Treaty and the settlement of relationships between the Federal Republic and other members of the Warsaw Pact. This has not only been said by both partners — the Federal Republic of Germany and the Soviet Union: Herr Barzel represented it as the Opposition's opinion in a letter to me in Bonn at the beginning of the week, before we flew to Moscow. So the Opposition sees this connection, too.

Given this connection, we do not need to discover an additional West Berlin question because, viewed politically, it is already contained in this connection. How can anyone regulate the relationship between the Federal Republic of Germany and the German Democratic Republic without including what has been agreed with respect to Berlin and West Berlin by the Four Powers? Who, just as we do, wish to establish their vital political interest? Our concept with regard to this question has been patiently, but also quite clearly developed and I have the impression that this has not escaped attention.

I feel strengthened in the opinion that I expressed before the microphone in Bonn prior to our flight — rather prematurely as it turned out: I could have said it a few hours later — that the Treaty would also exercise a favourable influence on this problem, in which our interest is also vital. I have good reason for this.

The Basis for a Peaceful Future

Declaration over radio and television concerning the German-Polish Treaty on November 20th, 1970.

Ladies and gentlemen,

Fellow countrymen,

The Treaty between the Federal Republic of Germany and the People's Republic of Poland is a moving document for both peoples.

It is to close a dark chapter of European history. It is to open a new one. The time has come to draw a line and start anew.

More than thirty years have passed since the Second World War began with the German attack. The Polish people had to endure untold suffering.

The war and its consequences have imposed infinite sacrifices on both nations, on us Germans, too. Now it is a matter of shaping a peaceful future for our two countries and peoples.

Those who have lost relatives, those who have been deprived of their homeland will find it hard to forget. And we others must understand and respect a burden they carry for all of us.

Yet, in this very hour, I must ask those of our countrymen who have been expelled from their native homes, not to persist in bitterness but to look ahead to the future.

It means a great deal that many families now have the prospect of receiving in their midst relatives from whom they have been separated for many years, and that it should be possible for them to revisit the birthplaces and graves of their ancestors in their former homeland.

I am in favour of the Treaty with the People's Republic of Poland because it creates the foundation for a peaceful future. It offers us the chance for understanding and co-operation.

To the Polish people the Treaty gives the assurance that they can live within secure boundaries. And as far as we are concerned, it should enable the principle of renunciation of force to be applied in all of Europe.

Only history will tell whether, as we hope, this will mark the beginning of real reconciliation such as, in the West, we have fortunately achieved with our neighbour France.

The Treaty does not of course mean the retrospective legitimation of injustice. It does, therefore, not mean the justification of expulsion.

What we want a quarter of a century after the war, is to make a serious attempt at putting a political end to the chain of injustice.

And as regards Poland's western frontier: that there can be neither détente nor secure peace in Europe unless — and, by the way, without touching the rights of the Four Powers with regard to Germany — we proceed from the situation as it is, as it has now been for twenty-five years.

It is not that, today, our nation is abruptly required to make a sacrifice. It had to make it long ago as a consequence of Hitler's crimes.

My Government says what most people in this country have been thinking in recent years.

And we can only hope that this will constitute an inspiring step towards a better Europe. A Europe where frontiers will no longer separate.

That is what the youth of our countries expects. We would wish to spare them, if possible, the burden of the past. We want to begin anew, for their sake.

We Must Break the Chain of Injustice

Remarks made on television in Warsaw on December 7th, 1970.

My dear fellow-countrymen,

I am conscious that this has been a difficult journey to make, but it is one that will be of consequence for a peaceful future. The Treaty of Warsaw is intended to draw a line under the sufferings and sacrifices of an evil past. It is intended to build a bridge between the two States and their peoples. It is to open up the way for separated families to reunite and to make frontiers less divisive than hitherto.

And yet, one could not have signed this Treaty without having earnestly examined one's conscience. We did not take this decision lightheartedly. We are fraught with memories, with blighted hopes. But our conscience is clear for we are convinced that tensions will have to be eliminated, treaties on the renunciation of force complied with, relations improved, and suitable forms of co-operation found, in order to achieve a European peace system.

In pursuing these aims we must start from what actually exists and from what has developed. This also applies with regard to the western frontier of Poland. Nobody has compelled us to see it this way; we have come of age. The point now ist to prove that we are mature and have the courage to recognize reality.

What I said when I spoke to you from Moscow, my dear fellow-countrymen, also holds true for the treaty with Poland: it does not surrender anything that was not gambled away long ago. Gambled away not by us who hold and held political responsibility in the Federal Republic of Germany, but gambled away by a criminal regime, by National Socialism.

We must not forget that what was inflicted on the Polish people after 1939 was the worst it had ever had to suffer in the course of its history. This injustice has had its consequences.

Our nation, too, was afflicted with great sorrow, especially our East German countrymen. We must be just: the greatest sacrifices have been made by those whose fathers, sons or brothers lost their lives. But next to them, it is those who had to leave their homeland who paid most severely for the war.

I refuse to accept legends, whether German or Polish: the history of the eastern regions of Germany cannot be arbitrarily rewritten. Our Polish partners know what I should like to tell you at home once again in all clarity: this Treaty does not mean that we recog-

The Federal Chancellor has friendly ties with the President of Zambia, Kenneth Kaunda, as shown here in discussion with Brandt and the Federal Foreign Minister, Herr Walter Scheel.

The President of the 24th General Assembly of the United Nations, Mrs. Angie Brooks-Randolph, visited West Germany during her term of office. She informed the Chancellor of forthcoming debates on outstanding problems in the General Assembly.

An important step in the Chancellor's efforts towards peace was the signing of the German-Soviet Treaty in Moscow. The Chancellor was greeted at the airport in Moscow by Prime Minister Kossygin.

On the occasion of the signing of the Treaty on the 12th of August 1970, the leading politicians of both nations posed for pictures: From left to right — Foreign Minister Scheel, Prime Minister Kossygin, Chancellor Brandt, Party Chief Brezhnev.

nize injustice or justify acts of violence. It does not mean that we subsequently legitimate expulsion.

Resentment offends the respect for the grief that mourns what has been lost — lost "in sorrow, war and alas, in unquenched tears," as the Silesian, Andreas Gryphius, put it at the end of the Thirty Years' War. No one can escape this grief. We are distressed by what has been lost and the hard-tried nation will respect our affliction.

Names like Auschwitz will be in the minds of both nations for a long time to come and will remind us that hell on earth is possible — we have experienced it. But this very experience constrains us to tackle the problems of the future with resolution. Escape from reality creates dangerous illusions. I therefore say: To subcribe to this Treaty, to reconciliation, and to peace, is to accept German history in its entirety.

A clear consciousness of history does not tolerate unrealizable claims. Nor does it tolerate those "secret reservations" which the East Prussian, Immanuel Kant, warns against in his essay "Towards Eternal Peace."

We must look to the future and see morals as a political force. We must break the chain of injustice. By so doing we are pursuing a policy not of surrender but of reason.

The Treaty between Poland and ourselves — a treaty, as the official title reads, concerning the Basis for Normalizing their Mutual Relations — is not a substitute for a formal peace treaty. It does not affect the rights and responsibilities of the Four Powers with regard to Germany as a whole. It does not deprive of effect any contractual obligations previously assumed by either side.

I wish to make special mention of this because naturally our active participation in the West European Communities and our firm place in the Atlantic Alliance form the basis from which we shall seek a new and better relationship with the peoples of Eastern Europe.

Not until we see the Treaty in this overall context does it become clear what it means for peace, for the divided German nation, and for a united Europe. A Europe which can be created not by declamations but by purposeful work only.

Nothing is more important than the creation of stable peace. There is no alternative. Peace is not possible without European solidarity. Everything that brings us closer to this objective will be a service to our nation, and above all to those who come after us.

German Policy is Directed Towards Peace and Understanding

The Federal Government's Report on the State of the Nation to the Bundestag on January 28th, 1971.

Mr. President, ladies and gentlemen,
This government is now making its second report on the position in divided Germany. At the same time, this High House has been presented with the Federal Government's answer to a major question from the S.P.D. and F.D.P. Parties on foreign policy.

As I promised here before the end of last year, papers intended to facilitate a comparison of conditions in the Federal Republic of Germany and the G.D.R. in various important fields have also been put at the disposal of this House in connection with the report on the State of the Nation.

I.

Ladies and gentlemen, in our reply to this major question — which the Government will explain in detail in the course of the following debate — the political tendencies and conditions are described which result from the state of the Federal Republic and which affect our country from outside. The state of affairs in Germany cannot, of course, be judged independently either of general international or European tendencies. So it is appropriate to clarify the significant events of 1970, to re-emphasize our working principles and to re-examine the attitudes of our allies.

Our reply to the major question states that our Eastern policy has the unanimous support of our allies. The fact that the leading representatives of the allied powers have not confined the expression of their support to confidential discussions has given us all the more encouragement to continue on the road that we regard as necessary. Our policy has been expressly supported in conferences of the West European communities and the Atlantic Alliance. I can take it that the published communiqués are well known to you.

As you know, I was in Paris at the beginning of this week, together with the Foreign Minister and other Cabinet colleagues. We were reminded once again of the friendly understanding which accompanies our efforts. "France supports you unreservedly," President Pompidou said in his speech, which — a noble gesture which we should not forget — was made in German. These latest talks in France have made abundantly clear the interdependence of our Western and Eastern policies and how much they belong together. In other words: West European cooperation and union — which, as everyone knows, we are actively encouraging — do not prevent us from developing better relations with the East; they are indeed the basis for such — we are convinced — necessary efforts.

Our policies directed towards reduction of tensions and the organization of peace are being followed with great interest and understanding by many governments, influential personalities and the Press in neutral countries and in wide areas of the Third World. Many people know that Europe will be able to achieve more in the field of international cooperation if these efforts lead to success.

Even in the eastern world, it is today hardly doubted that German policy is directed towards peace. And it is known that we are making no exceptions, not even in the case of the G.D.R., in our efforts to reach understanding.

Seen from this point of view, it was only logical, when signing the Moscow Treaty on the 12th August last year, to declare our agreement with the Soviet Union that all treaties we may want to conclude with the partners of the Warsaw Pact will form a political whole.

No one will be able to speak of effective relaxation of tension in Central Europe until all these elements are present.

Over and above this, I want to establish here that these treaties — to be exact, the treaty with the Soviet Union and that with the People's Republic of Poland — in no way contradict our position as a member of the European Community or as an ally of N.A.T.O. In neither West nor East, North nor South are there particular German interests or special German reservations, which could diminish or influence our decision in favour of a policy of settlement. However, we made it clear in Moscow that no treaty either can or may prevent us from striving for a state of peace in which our nation can recover its unity in freedom and self-determination. This reflects the task laid down in our constitution as well as our own convictions. But no one believes that aspirations come any nearer to fulfilment by being committed to paper.

We also have German interests in the widest sense at heart in our relationship to Poland, in doing what we can to ensure that the name of Germany shall no longer be used as a symbol of injustice and horror, but as a sign of hope for reconciliation and peaceful coexistence. That this hope is not in vain may be seen in the number of Germans who will cross to the Federal Republic in the coming months.

With regard to relations with the G.D.R.: as laid down in the principles of the United Nations regarding relations between states, peaceful settlement of relations on the basis of human rights, equality, peaceful coexistence and non-discrimination must occupy the foreground of all efforts in this case as well.

The meetings at Erfurt and Kassel were important for the neighbourly coexistence of the two systems of government on German soil, even though they were only the beginning of a discussion. We consequently reached an arrangement with the Government of the G.D.R., at the end of October, to conduct an official exchange of opinions on questions whose settlement would serve the cause of relaxation of tension in Central Europe and which are of interest to both states.

We stand by all this. Here is a basis, which is not bound by any pre-condition and on which we can work in 1971. We were not to blame for the fact that the first talks between the State Secretaries to be held on the basis of this agreement were marred by delay. The fourth of these meetings took place on Tuesday this week and there will probably be many more before we can speak of the positive results we desire. However, I regard it as a sign of progress that these discussions are losing their initial tinge of sensationalism.

The 20 Points which I communicated to the Chairman of the G.D.R. Ministerial Council, Herr Stoph, in Kassel on 21st May, 1970, remain the guideline for our ideas of how equality of relations can be objectively settled. The G.D.R. gives priority to traffic questions. This is interesting and we are prepared to discuss all outstanding problems in this field, about a comprehensive treaty or about mutual agreements. As far as problems of Berlin traffic are concerned, however, we shall not anticipate the basic agreements of the Four Powers.

This survey of developments since my last report a year ago makes clear the extent to which the settlement of relations between the Federal Republic of Germany and the G.D.R. must be seen in relation to the whole. An isolated solution to the problems affecting our people is just as impossible as, say, an attempt to secure peace on our own. History has taught us that crises can be created by one, but the maintenance of peace requires the cooperation of all.

What is possible between the states of Europe must also be possible between the two states in Germany; the artificial severance which has now lasted more than two decades has brought neither stability nor transquillity. On the contrary, it has aroused tensions and crises which must now be overcome in the interests of Europe and Germany.

Nobody knows whether — even in comparison to the present thoroughly unsatisfactory situation for our people — there may not be further setbacks to come. We may exercise an influence on external events, but their influence on us is considerably stronger. Nevertheless, we should not allow ourselves to be dissuaded from attempting to break down the policy of confrontation fostered above all by the leadership of the S.E.D. (Socialist Unity Party of the G.D.R.), the cost of which, in the long run, is borne by the people. This people justifiably demands that those problems capable of settlement now should in fact be tackled.

In doing this, we are starting from realities. We are neither stipulating pre-conditions nor setting up insurmountable obstacles. Our efforts are based simply on the self-evident fact that relaxation of tension in Europe cannot exclude an area in the centre of Europe: it cannot exclude the Federal Republic of Germany or Berlin or the G.D.R.

1970 has seen the return of the German question to the agenda of European and international politics, in a partly new form but certainly with greater urgency. What has been started must now be consistently and patiently pursued.

II.

This is the rough framework in which we should examine the state of the nation.

In the interests of a better understanding of the internal situation in the two states which make up the Germany of 1970/71, the Federal Government has provided the Bundestag and the Bundesrat with papers, in which an attempt is made to compare developments here and in the G.D.R. These papers are the result of work by a group of experts under the leadership of Professor Christian Ludz. Although engaging in constant consultations with the relevant government departments, the group carried out its research independently and autonomously, using scientific methods.

The group concentrated its work on areas of life which are inherently connected but which are also basically suited to a well-grounded empiric comparison in accordance with current methods of research and statistics. The areas chosen on this basis, which range from population and industrial structure to various economic and social fields, including the situation of youth, are closely connected with three important questions in the competition of the systems existing in the two parts of Germany, namely: with the consciousness of being industrial performance-orientated societies, with growth and modernization of the respective systems and with the increasing importance of science and research, of specialist and scientific training.

Various factors have been ascertained which are or will be of considerable significance to the people in divided Germany. However, it must be clearly and firmly stated that comparison does not mean equalization; the sober presentation of data does not imply approval of the political ideology and social conditions in the other half of Germany. This understood, such investigations should be continued and intensified; their value lies not so much in the presentation of facts as such as in their use and the deductions reached by those with political responsibility. Where the state of the nation is concerned, the contribution of science should assist political judgement and bring objectivity to political discussion. In any case, I hope these "papers" will receive due attention, not only in the debate of this High House, but also among the general public and in scientific, political and educational work, and that future projects will be encouraged by means of criticism and suggestions.

I would like to express here my acknowledgement of the work done by the members of this expert commission. My thanks go particularly to Federal Minister Egon Franke, who seized the initiative of forming the commission and supervised and encouraged its research.

In examining the state of our divided nation, as clearly expressed in these "papers," one should not make the mistake of regarding Germany's current problems as being solely the result of the creation of two German states in 1949. The origins lie, as we know, much further back. I would like to remind you here of what I said in my government policy statement on 28th October, 1969:

"This government believes that the problems resulting for the German people from the Second World War and the national betrayal by the Hitler Regime can only be finally resolved in a European peace settlement. No one, however, can dissuade us that the Germans have the same right to self-determination as all other peoples. The task of practical policy in the years which lie ahead of us is to uphold the unity of the nation by freeing relations between the two parts of Germany from their present state of rigidity."

And in my last speech on the state of the nation a year ago, on 14th January, 1970, I added:

"25 years after the unconditional capitulation of Hitler's Reich, the concept of nationhood binds divided Germany ... A nation is based on the continuous feeling of belonging together of people. No one can deny that, in this sense, there is a German nation and will continue to be one as far as we can see into the future." These conclusions formed the basis of my statements in Erfurt and Kassel and also the basis of the talks which the Foreign Minister and I and our colleagues conducted in Moscow and Warsaw. There could not and cannot be any question of ignoring the elements of our historical development for tactical, let alone opportunist reasons.

Nor is there any question for us of adjusting the concept of nationhood to apparently contemporary or short-term necessities. I have no hesitation in quoting a man who declared, inter alia, on 30th November, 1970:

„We are patriots and internationalists at one and the same time. For, whether one wants to believe it or not, the nation is a reality which will not disappear in the foreseeable future. If we are to achieve fruitful international relations between states, the nations must develop among themselves relations of cooperation, understanding and friendship. This means that we are firm opponents of what may be called national nihilism."

So much for the quotation. It stems from the Chairman of the Communist Party in France in the French Senate, Jacques Duclos, a man who surely needs no introduction to the leaders of the S.E.D.

Incidentally, he bases his concept of the "nation" on the classic communist thinkers. And one can find no word in his concept suggesting that only certain parts of the population form the nation or excluding the "class enemy" or those considered as such. It was left to the S.E.D. leadership to make a distinction between the "bourgeois nation" and the "socialist nation," whereby — strangely enough — it is said that "remains of the old bourgeois German nation" are preserved in the Federal Republic. To complicate things even further, since 1970 the G.D.R. has adopted the terms "socialist state of the German nation" and "socialist German national state," thereby both confirming and denying the continuance of one German nation. These observations and indications show how difficult discussions are when the partner wants to have and be two things at the same time. For whereas the G.D.R., pointing to the "socialist German national state," declares that there can be no "special relations" between the two German states, the same leadership claims the right to undertake what it calls "an offensive policy of peaceful coexistence towards the F.R.G." With no other state in the world does the G.D.R. concern itself so thoroughly and so actively as with the Federal Republic.

And now I would ask: is this not the same intervention in the affairs of another state, otherwise so eagerly pilloried by the leadership of the G.D.R.? And does it not often go as far as encouraging our citizens to resist the internal order of their state?

I say this not only for the sake of necessary demarcation. I also want to make it clear that such conduct, negative though it be, shows a special interest in that part of the German nation living in the Federal Republic. Clearly, there is here an interest of a special kind and the involuntary documentation of the "special relations" otherwise denied. But this special interest is manifested in such a way that it makes the gulf between the two parts of Germany deeper than between other states with different ideological and social structures. Our common national basis leads the government in East Berlin not to playing down but to exaggerating the antitheses between East and West.

The other side frequently appeals to political realities. This is why we should now declare with all urgency: freedom, democracy and social justice are not formal concepts for us. They are the tasks laid down by our constitution, by the Basic Law, and they form the inalienable foundations of our political and social existence. We are ready to enter any contest concerned with more personal freedom and more social justice.

But there is one point on which we are in agreement with Herr Ulbricht, Chairmann of the State Council and First Secretary, when he speaks of demarcation: neither ideologically nor socially can there be any mixing of antitheses nor any minimization of differences of opinion; this is — unfortunately — specially true of the two states in Germany, which belong to such different systems. But even these two states must be able to achieve a form of peaceful coexistence in which neither holds the other in tutelage, but both provide an example abroad that even between such different political and social systems, peaceful cooperation is possible.

Nationhood is a question of consciousness and will. The polemics of East Berlin against the nation confirm the existence of this consciousness and will, which have also been preserved over there to a great extent. Differing interpretations of this theme need not hinder efforts for a settled, objective coexistence of the two German states. However, both sides must respect the fact that the Four Powers hold and will continue to hold responsibility for Germany as a whole and for Berlin. This situation is not an obstacle to the intentions of the Federal Government to reach with the G.D.R. agreements setting out clear obligations, such as are normal and necessary between states.

The government in East Berlin has considered it right to defame and throw doubts on our efforts towards peaceful coexistence and the settlement of material problems. The Federal Government will not let itself be deterred by this; we hold to the view that the G.D.R.'s international relations will encounter less obstacles when necessary adjustments to the situations on Germany itself have been achieved.

We are concerned with alleviation and improvements for people in both German states in their mutual relations and we are also concerned with the common responsibility of Germans for peace in Europe and the world. This is not a pronouncement made with a raised forefinger, it is an honest and necessary pointer to the theme of national responsibility.

III.

With no other subject are the problematics of the state of our nation so clear at present as with Berlin. Double division, German responsibilities, competencies sometimes of the Three, sometimes of the Four Powers form the complicated factors of the actual position.

When we speak of relaxation of tension in Central Europe, relaxation of the position in and around Berlin must of necessity be included. The attitude of the Federal Government on this has always been clear. It was publicly formulated on the 7th June last year with respect to negotiations with the Soviet Union, as follows:

"It is assumed that the Four Power negotiations will lead to securing the close connection between the Federal Republic of Germany and West Berlin. Without this being secured, a treaty on the renunciation of violence cannot be put into force."

So much for the quotation from the Federal Government's resolution on the 7th June last year.

I am reminding you of this in order to add: the Federal Government holds to its standpoint. As it has pointed out again and again to the interested parties, it will not dispense with this material connection.

It should be remembered that the Berlin talks, which have since developed into negotiations began on Western initiative in summer 1969. The impulse was given by a pronouncement of the President of the United States of America during his visit to Berlin at the begin of 1969. He said then to the employees of the Siemens Works — and here I quote:

"When we say that we reject any unilateral alteration of the status quo in Berlin, it does not mean that we regard the status quo as satisfactory ... Let us, all of us, regard the situation in Berlin as an appeal to action, as a challenge to end the tensions of a past age, here and everywhere in the world. Our common bearing is best expressed by a quotation from Goethe: Ohne Hast, doch ohne Rast. Without haste, yet without rest. Step by step, we shall attempt together to create a lasting peace."

For those who are so greatly concerned about "haste," that was not yesterday but, as I said, in February 1969, and now we have January 1971. President Nixon went on to say:

"In the past, there were times when Berlin had to stand up to powerful forces which threatened to overwhelm it. Your determination" — this was addressed to the Berliners — "in those times of danger has proved beyond doubt that threats and force will never be successful. Through your strength, you have created conditions which, at the appropriate time, may permit another kind of determination — a determination that, by means of negotiations of governments with each other and reconciliation among the people, an end will be prepared to the division of this city, this nation, this continent and this planet."

Now, we have been negotiating for some time — as I said — as to how and whether, irrespective of certain basic unnegotiable positions, a satisfactory Berlin settlement can be reached. It has been and continues to be a matter of course for the Federal Government to maintain close contact with the three Western powers on the positions to be taken up. I can state here that cooperation with the four Western governments has in recent months and particularly in this field gained an intensity seldom experienced before. There exists complete agreement on the criteria and content required of a Berlin settlement if it is to be satisfactory both in our sense and in that of the Western powers.

These include requirements which were strongly impressed on me in my years as Governing Mayor of Berlin. I must be quite frank with you, ladies and gentlemen: at one time I wanted a common political effort by all concerned, by means of which Berlin would have become a province of the Federal Republic of Germany — in accordance with our constitution — and I supported this cause. Things have developed differently, but not in such a way that Berlin could become a so-called "independent political unit." What are important today are the ties that have grown up, the feelings of close solidarity. And saying this gives me the welcome opportunity to mention the good cooperation and full understanding with the Berlin Senate, which is taking a constructive part in all required considerations.

At this point I would like to thank the three Western powers and their heads of government for their understanding, which is expressed in principles as well as in practical daily work. And above all for their recognition of the Federal Republic's supremely vital interest in West Berlin. This may be written into agreements, but the decisive thing is the resulting practical harmonization of interests.

I can also state that the Federal Government's expectation that the Moscow Treaty would further and intensify the Berlin negotiations is justified. We still, of course, have no actual legal title with respect to the Four Powers, but even the Soviet side no longer disputes our vital interest in a satisfactory Berlin settlement.

I will say no more, but this much I do say because it belongs in the stock-taking of January 1971.

The Four Powers agreed on special privacy for the Berlin negotiations. The Federal Government, which is actively supporting these negotiations in every way possible, has consented to this condition. It has therefore had to exercise restraint in public discussion, although it has great understanding for the lively public interest in the progress of the negotiations.

In such a situation, misunderstandings are sometimes unavoidable — as I know. However, on the whole it has been possible to maintain a high degree of accordance in approaching the Berlin problem between the Government, the Coalition parties and the Opposition. It would be good if we could continue like this in the common interest and for the sake of Berlin.

The Federal Government agrees with the powers concerned with Berlin that such extraordinarily complicated negotiations, which must take into account the results of over twenty years' development, should not be subject to pressures of time. At the same time, the work should go forward briskly, so that the negotiations, once they have reached a point at which it seems appropriate, can be further developed and take on the character of conferences. I am not going to make any forecasts as to timing. But I will try to summarize the goal briefly: the Berlin Settlement must take account of the realities that exist, that is, it must make West Berlin as trouble-free as humanly possible by means of unlimited agreements between East and West, thereby initiating peaceful development of the city for the future. Berlin, the symbol of Cold War conflict, must become a symbol of respected coexistence and collaboration in the centre of a peacefully cooperating Europe.

The Federal Government — and, I am sure, this whole House — utterly condemns the difficulties and hindrances on the roads to Berlin. This is a fruitless attempt to demonstrate factual competencies which is aimed at exercising pressure. Obstruction of the access routes is obstruction of the negotiations.

It is obvious that the government of the G.D.R. is using ever new pretexts to exacerbate the situation just when negotiations are in progress, the aim of which, among other things, is to agree on unhindered access. In my opinion, our reply can only be a political one: there will be no Berlin settlement that does not guarantee the right of free assembly just as much as unhindered access.

The Federal Government is in close contact with the Three Powers that bear special responsibility for all questions connected with Berlin. Within this framework, it remains the Federal Government's task to devote particular attention to the economic situation of West Berlin. Even if the security of the city and its access routes are the responsibility of the Three Powers, we ourselves still bear a large measure of responsibility for the viability of the city; there is no one who has this more at heart than a Federal Chancellor who bore considerable political responsibility for Berlin during a whole decade.

Looking back over the past year, the Federal Government and all of us here together, the Federal Government and the Bundestag, have taken further effective measures to obviate the difficulties inherent in the situation of the city as far as possible. In this connection, I would remind you of the new draft of the Berlin Assistance Act which came into force during the year and also of the Guiding Principles for the Promotion of Employment in West Berlin. In both these cases, there are important new regulations for employees and employers. Efforts to promote labour and economic growth continued to be successful in 1970.

If the political situation improves, this will also have a positive effect on the economy. The safeguarding of Berlin's position will — when we have reached this stage — enable the city to augment its special contribution to economic and cultural exchange in Germany and in Europe.

IV.

The division of Germany inherited from the War also struck hard on some areas this side of the border; what had been a heartland became a fringe area remote from the economic centre. Historic, political, cultural and economic ties were broken.

In accordance with a resolution by the German Bundestag on 2nd July, 1953, successive federal governments have repeatedly stressed their intentions of giving priority to this inner-German fringe area. This Government has presented the House with the draft of a Bill aimed at coordinating previous promotional measures and preferences for the affected areas. It also foresees considerable improvements in the fields of housing and social facilities.

A further 80 million DM are to be set aside from the Federal Budget, whereby future plans will concentrate not only on economic promotion but also on measures to improve the infrastructure.

V.

In our efforts to the best of our ability to render the results of the division of Germany more bearable to all those affected, I am thinking particularly today of the large group of our population who lost their old homelands 25 years ago as a result of the war.

Nobody should presume to disparage those who still today suffer pain and sadness over the loss of their homelands in the East. They bore a heavier burden than many other Germans. Yet is was their delegates who, 20 years ago in the Charter of Stuttgart, abjured hate and sought for settlement with our eastern neighbours. That Charter was a document of humanity and reason, which turned its gaze to the future and expressed a clear rejection of the barbaric methods of the past.

Certain people now want to awaken an impression among the exiles that a real possibility of return has been lost through the Treaty we have signed with Poland, that their real exile dates from now and that a renunciation of attainable rights has taken place. On this occasion, I would just like to say the following:

— If today we are willing for the sake of peace to proceed from the existing borders in Europe, that is also those in Eastern Europe, and to respect them, this does not by any means imply a legitimation or silent approval of the eviction of Germans from these areas that took place in 1945 and 1946. We have not just lost the war today — as we all know — and there has been plenty of time to orientate ourselves and obtain information on the attitude of foreign powers, including our closest allies.

— We want to break down barriers — and not just through this Treaty — between the German and Polish peoples, barriers resulting from a difficult historical heritage and particularly from the Second World War.

— Among the losses of eviction were not just the bases of material existence; we are concerned with an area which brought forth great achievements and contributions to German cultural and intellectual life. The Federal Government will assist in fostering this cultural heritage.

— As far as material losses are concerned, the Federal Republic has not even approched full compensation. However, in most cases economic assimilation has been successful. Personal ability and skill and also the favourable economic development of our Federal Republic have played their part in this.

Nevertheless, I ask our citizens who have not had to pay for the war with the loss of their homeland and all its inestimable associations to give their understanding and help to all those who still do not feel quite at home here.

— Following the conclusion of the treaty with Poland, many families can look forward to receiving their relations now living there. As you know, the first small groups are already arriving in the Federal Republic. Adjustment to life here will at first not be easy for some of these people. The Federal Government and the Länder governments will do everything in their power to help; but we need the cooperation of everyone to ease the burdens of acclimatization and a new start for these Germans who are coming to us.

Furthermore, I appeal to all citizens of the Federal Republic, men and women alike — whatever their origins, to play their part in seeing that the reconciliation with the Polish people becomes a lasting reality. The same applies in our efforts to achieve a settlement with the peoples of Czechoslovakia and to all reconciliation and cooperation with the East.

VI.

Our efforts to normalize relations with the East European states and the other part of Germany have led in past months not only to legitimate differences of opinion on content and form — as they will also be expressed in this House — but also to very vehement actions on the part of small groups whose volume has borne and bears no relation to their numbers. These groups, which are trying — under the misused and in this case macabre slogan of "resistance" — to exploit some of the exiles for their aims, represent neither the policy of our country nor the will of the people. They consist of a residue of radical organizations who are constantly trying out new methods of attracting dissatisfied citizens to their contemptible purposes.

We know what effect such campaigns, set against the background of history, have on our neighbours and on our friends in the West. The evil committed under the Hitler regime has left deep scars, not only in the public opinion of neighbouring countries. We may prefer to dismiss exaggerated reaction in these countries, but we must try to understand it even if it is not justified by the facts.

The Federal Government believes that the overwhelming majority of our population rejects the aims and methods of the groups just mentioned, all the more so as many of our citizens still remember how destructive such forces can be. In any case, recent elections have clearly demonstrated that our people is not willing to entrust itself to extremists and obvious political adventurers.

We must defend ourselves energetically against those — whichever side they may come from — who wish to make violence or terror an instrument of political confrontation. And nationalistic agitation is forbidden both by bitter experience and the principles of our free constitution.

VII.

It has been said and written that, in view of events in Europe, the first year of this new decade is seen by some people as a kind of "German year." In the old Berlin manner, I would ask whether we might not have it "a size smaller." In any case, we should not forget that others have been involved in these efforts. However, we can say without complacency that in these difficult efforts to secure peace — and they are still difficult — the Federal Republic of Germany has not been a silent partner but a driving force and will continue to be so. This also applies to Western, especially West European cooperation with our Eastern neighbours.

Our policy does not suffer from a lack of balance. The promotion of West European cooperation, the further development of the Atlantic Alliance and the cultivation of trusted friendships remain the foundations of our policy. We stand with both feet firmly in the Western community. Close and indissoluble partnership with our friends and allies is not only the basis of our common efforts towards the pacification of Europe, it is of grat value in itself.

On the other hand we cannot and do not want to rest content with this, any more than our partners in the West. In this process, with its ultimate aim of relaxing tension in Europe, the Federal Republic has taken over an appointed but independent role. Important as it is to go hand in hand with our Western partners, it is just as clear that a number of barriers and obstacles can only be cleared away by Germans, by ourselves. If we are to make a fresh start, we ourselves must deal with a major part of the inheritance of the war begun and lost by the Third Reich. The overcoming of European tensions is also dependent on our own contribution, especially with regard to the establishment of a tolerable contractual relationship between the two states in Germany. This is a task of which nobody can relieve us; we must tackle it ourselves.

In summing up, I want to affirm that we are proceeding on the basis of the following facts and expectations:

1. The right to self-determination laid down in the United Nations Charter must be conceded to the Germans in the historical process.

2. The German nation remains a reality, even if divided into differing state and social systems.
3. The policy of the Federal Republic of Germany, which is pledged to the preservation of peace, requires a contractual settlement of relations with the G.D.R. The principles and contractual elements established in the 20 Points of Kassel remain our valid basis for negotiations.
4. The judicial status of Berlin may not be called in question. In the framework of the rights and undertakings approved by the Three Powers responsible, the Federal Republic of Germany will do its part to ensure that the viability of West Berlin is better safeguarded than previously.
5. A satisfactory result of the Four Power negotiations on the improvement of the situation in and around Berlin will enable the Federal Government to present the treaty signed in Moscow on 12th August, 1970, to the legislative bodies for ratification.
6. The same timing and political connection applies to the decision of the legislative bodies on the treaty signed in Warsaw on 7th December, 1970, with the People's Republic of Poland.

I have tried to report objectively, for I am convinced that we can only do justice to the state of the nation if we are capable of conducting the exchange of opinion in a manner fitting to the matter in hand and to our responsibility.

Chancellor Brandt on signing the German-Soviet Treaty.

The conversations with the General Secretary of the Communist Party, Leonid Brezhnev, which began in 1970, were continued by Chancellor Brandt during his visit to the Crimean peninsula in September 1971.

A few months after signing the Treaty in Moscow Chancellor Brandt and the Chairman of the Council of Ministers of the People's Republic of Poland, Joseph Cyrankiewicz, set their signatures to the German-Polish Treaty in Warsaw on 7th December 1970. The document represents reconciliation with the Polish people.

Chancellor Brandt knelt before the Memorial Stone in the Warsaw Ghetto in remembrance of the millions of victims of Fascist domination.

Confrontation and Cooperation

Speech at a ceremony of the American Council on Germany in New York in memory of June 17th, 1953.

The circle in which we are today in New York has a tradition which I would like to continue. It is a circle where one meets friends. There are people here who for the Federal Republic of Germany and for Berlin have done great service for the relations between our two states and peoples. I see faces in front of me, with whom I have been acquainted for many years and who are known and recognized as true friends in my country.

And these friends in particular are asking the question on this day: What remains of the experiences which we collected in the postwar years? What remains — in connection with the present day — of that which links us with the memory of June 17th, 1953? You can further ask whether our present policy — the policy of alliance, of the West Europeans, of the Federal Government — has not distanced itself from knowledge gained on a common basis earlier. Whether the present policy is not perhaps in conflict to ideas which we have developed together, to ideals which are common to us all.

Now let me say without beating about the bush: June 17th was in 1953 already a difficult day: when the working people demonstrated for better working conditions and free elections; when the streets bore banners; when the Soviet tanks drove up; when a state of emergency was imposed; when my people held their fists clenched in their pockets and people looked across from West Berlin; When there was still no war; when the protective powers also looked on and could do nothing else because of their concern for peace.

June 17th has remained a difficult day. Those who have experienced this day in East Berlin and in the GDR among the endless chain of nameless days work today as on any other day. Those in the Federal Republic, who read about the events of June 17th in the newspaper the next day are pleased about since their holiday. One is almost afraid to say it but it is true; what came from the victims of others is what we call "sozialen Besitzstand."

Nobody can be more deeply convinced than we who have political responsibility in the Federal Republic of Germany, that history is not extinguished. That is in part a burden. It is in this case an encouraging certainty.

What Western Europe became again after 1945, it became through the help and the protection of the United States. And this applies particularly to the Federal Republic of Germany. The Marshall Plan made it possible to establish a functioning economy out of the ruins. The Atlantic Alliance gave it protection. Security and economic growth form the basis to obtain a place in international politics inwardly and outwardly. This part of our history is also something we cannot lose.

When one asks oneself what has changed in the last one and a half centuries, one finds; doubtless important developments have occurred, but certain basic conditions have remained unchanged. Western Europe becomes stronger. It is on the way to an expanded economic community which will also lead to close political cooperation. In East and West relations, confrontation has become easier and a limited balance appears possible. But the basic facts in the relations between Western Europe and the United States exist now as ever: both need each other, today just as twenty years ago. Both need the balance of power in the relations with the Eastern world. In my view, the principle agreement of interests — and after decades of partnership also essential convictions — reduces partial difficulties to the right extent.

We in Germany enjoy the protection of a world power and have understanding for the concerns of a world power. We also have understanding for the fact that the United States want to disemburden and that the American economy wants to have no disadvantages from the EEC. West European union — which is now making progress at last after years of stagnation — may not lead to a cutting off of Western Europe. This lies in the common interest. And I am sure that wie shall find solutions to overcome the inevitable difficulties.

West European Union will increase the political weight of Western Europe. Western Europe will try, and has already begun to do so, to harmonize the views of its members on political questions. The Community is developing into one partner who wants to speak in the course of this century increasingly with one voice. It will then bear political coresponsibility which will lead in the long-term also to a reduction of the burdens of the United States.

I want to point out that the Atlantic Alliance has not become weaker in the last few years, but that its inner holding together has increased. Politically agreement was reached two or more years ago that effective defence and the striving to overcome tensions are two sides of the same medal. And last year, important principles arose to strengthen the practical responsibility of the European partners within the Alliance.

Taking our point of departure, there is a broader field which can lead to common disemburdenment. The military balance will not be indispensable as a guarantee for Europe, but it can be perhaps achieved in stages. It is a question of the guaranteed reduction of dangers. We have already for years had negotiations on a reciprocal balance of troop strength on an equal basis and welcome the fact that preparations for negotiations on this have been introduced in the Alliance. We divide up the burden of military efforts which remain an imperative requisite for promising negotiations. We also want to divide the burden in the case of successful negotiations.

This subject can naturally not be divided from the attempts between the United States and the Soviet Union to reach a limitation of armaments efforts in the first place in the field of strategic defence weapons. Those who see connections in world-political terms will ascertain that the politics of my government are neither a single step of their own nor rivalry, but that they constitute a logical supplement and continuation, for which our allies are striving. The aim is to render the necessary German contribution to a détente between East and West.

Our policy is not limited to applauding others when they speak about peace. We ask ourselves what can be done to disband tensions, to open up fields of down-to-earth cooperation and thus make peace more secure.

I think it is necessary to think explicitly of two things:

1. that our efforts to achieve East European treaties are a consequence of the Western treaties concluded in the fifties and the experiences which had to be made in the sixties with confrontation;
2. that the efforts of the Federal Republic are embedded in efforts of its partners and friends moving in the same direction.

The Federal Republic of Germany is now catching up to a certain extent with the normalization of its relations to the states of Eastern Europe, which its allies have already done. It respects that the frontiers run in the way that they do at present. It recognizes that there is a political West just as there is a political East: that there are social systems which cannot be mixed. It is conscious that there is an undeniable delineation between democracy and communism. And that finally, as painful as it is for us, the partition of the German nation can only be overcome in so far as the partition of Europe can be overcome. In this, as has been said, painful recognition, there is agreement between the government and opposition in the Federal Republic of Germany. We shall this year have to remember for the tenth time August 13th, without anything having changed about the Wall in Berlin. Nothing has changed about its absurdity, about its abnormality, about its horror and its existence. That which lies behind that wall is a part of Berlin, a part of Germany, and has nevertheless become a state of its own. We have come to the result that not only an attitude to the division of Germany was needed in the past. We protested against it and that was right. We shall do it again. We have defended ourselves against it and that was our right. We have complained about it and that remains understandable. But all that is not enough. The running against walls becomes senseless, when they are made of international cement. The protest or the complaint become embarrassing, if they end in self-pity or in resignation. To overcome inhuman and unnecessary consequences of division is the challenge which we have to make ourselves. In the shadow of the Berlin negotiations, an exchange of views with the GDR has begun. Today, it cannot have as an object state unity. What will become of Germany as a whole depends on the future development between East and West and between the parts of Europe just as on the future will of the German people.

We are striving to regulate our relations with the GDR and this is the form of a binding nature between states. The meetings of Erfurt and Kassel last year did not lead to concrete results. The exchange of views between representatives of both governments, going out for some time, is down-to-earth, but nothing definite can be said about them.

That which has been announced by the GDR leaders as a programme of "complete delineation" with regard to the Federal Republic is certainly not helpful; it testifies neither to marked self-awareness. But because of that in particular I can say: The clearly apparent and ineffacable differences do not need to be a hindrance for the creation of relations governed by treaties which accord with the interests of both sides and all the people concerned. We are in any case prepared without effacing the differences to continue the process begun. From the ordering of the circumstances by treaty between the two states will result then their peaceful competition at an international level. Between both states in Germany, there must be at first at least as much in the way of relations as exists between other states of Western and Eastern Europe. The fact that the states on German soil have the worst relations — with a multitude of impediments which could be avoided — may not remain forever. The community of language, culture and history, but also responsibility for the future peace in Europe cannot separate in the long-term, but it raises responsibility for both sides. Both sides are thus faced objectively with the tasks which accrue for them.

We cannot succumb to illusions. Détente or even cooperation are not questions of a decision, which can be taken at once, but processes which need time. Only in theory, confrontation and cooperation can be excluded. In practice, they will exist alongside between East and West, in the world and in Germany for a long time. The controversy — politically and ideologically — will continue to determine policy in Europe and in Germany. We can fulfil our duty to Europe and to peace only in the framework of our alliance. And the GDR has its place in the military, economic and other connections of the Warsaw Pact.

A Polish journalist remarked recently that with the signing of the Moscow Treaty of August 12th the postwar period had come to an end. The chance to reach at least partial cooperation despite all the difficulties had never been so great for Europe as during the last twenty years. The task of both states in Germany is not to destroy this chance, not to emburden this process unnecessarily, but to make a specific contribution to it.

Our treaties with Moscow and Warsaw level the way here. The Soviet Union assumes the place in our efforts which accords with its political significance. But all our efforts and all our strivings by friends and allies would be doomed to failure, if it did not prove possible for the point in our European détente, which has symbolized tensions for a long time, Berlin, to have a part in this.

Berlin — that is the German capital, from which Hitler began his war, which brought unspeakable misfortune over Europe. Unspeakable misfortune also for my people. It is the city which has suffered the most horribly right up to the present day.

To mention Berlin means also to remind one's listeners of one of the strongest links which bind this country here and democratic Germany, that means awakening the memory of one of the great successes which Western determination and holding together achieved at a geographically unfavourable point.

The fact that this divided city lives and radiates is due to the guarantees of the United States and the British and French Allies for the integrity of Berlin, and of course just as much to the tenacity and vitality of the Berliners. The determination of all concerned is based on insight into the significance which Berlin has for Germany and for Europe, and furthermore for worldwide East-West-relations.

In the future also the existance of West Berlin will depend on just these factors. Earlier it was a matter of defending West Berlin. Now it is a matter for the first time for many years of improving the situation of West Berlin. In earlier times it was a question of being determined to guard the city. Today we are concerned with reaching agreement in our will to force through imperative regulations for the viability. I am convinced that we can do this.

The special rights of the three protective powers must remain untouched, also and in particular in the interest of West Berlin. The "three essentials," which President Kennedy formulated in 1961, must not only be stabilized, but there mutualization must be secured.

For all persons and goods, traffic between the Federal Republic of Germany and West Berlin must be untrammelled on the basis of binding agreements of the Four Powers and — rooted in — those of the German authorities concerned. The connections between West Berlin and the Federal Republic, which have grown up with the approval of the three powers, must remain upheld on ths basis of the situation which has developed and exists.

The West Berliners must again receive the opportunity to visit the Eastern part of the city and their surroundings.

We need an agreement, which after all the experience we have gathered, liberates Berlin from being a point of confrontation and dangerous crises. We need an agreement which without temporal connections gives the city a solid, secure future.

In earlier times the Germans stressed on this day their right of natural unity. There was too little talk about the European and international responsibility of the Germans. Historically speaking, the separation of Europe is a consequence of Hitler's war. It was against our wish, but it is reality, that the Germans live today in two states. This does not reduce their responsibility for peace in Europe. And thus this day is for the German Federal Chancellor the day of realizing his responsibility for what has to be done, so that the states in Europe may draw nearer together, can live with each other and alongside each other, with the German people among them and with them.

There are domains where we cannot have ourselves represented, but where the ice can only be broken by us. Thus a ceremonious declaration about the inviolability of the European frontiers, if it is expressed by the Federal Republic of Germany, has particular significance. Thus, the reconciliation with Poland is a specific — and I think moral — contribution to European peace. The particular relationship to the Soviet Union — not only as one of the powers responsible for Germany as a whole — requires special efforts from our point of view.

The policy of the Federal Republic of Germany was for a long time — and not without reason — exposed to the criticism that too little was done to promote détente in Europe. Since then we are sometimes asked, whether we have not perhaps done too much in an easterly direction. Let me say here:

We are striving to achieve the right measure and down-to-earth common sense. We are not chasing illusions and we are not sacrificing friendships which have proved themselves. But I think nevertheless that it was necessary and time twenty-five years af·ter the end of the war to begin to attempt to clear things up.

Let me say quite openly: as long as military means of power exist which explicitly or predominantly can stress the policy powers, then no peaceloving state can avoid protecting its independence and its territorial integrity by means of its own military efforts. We agree with our allies that military preparedness must go hand in hand with a policy of détente.

I am grateful for the fact that I may say this in New York today. Our friends can rely on us. Together we have withstood times of confrontation, together we have also passed through times of negotiations and together achieved a situation in which the word cooperation will be written in larger letters.

On the 25th Anniversary of the Founding of the United Nations

Statement by the Federal Chancellor on October 24th, 1970.

On October 24th, 1970, the United Nations Organization celebrates 25 years of existence.

This jubilee is of great importance to the Federal Republic of Germany. True, we have not yet attained full membership of the World Organization, but we are in the family of United Nations.

Not only does the Federal Government accord full acknowledgement to the principles of the United Nations, the Federal Republic has been an active member of the U.N. special organizations for twenty years and participates in all relief work, special projects and development programmes of the United Nations.

In view of the painful experiences of earlier decades, the people of Germany have a particular interest in aspiring to the high aims of the United Nations: understanding and cooperation between the nations of the world. The Federal Government is making every effort towards the progressive realization of the great tasks of peace and cooperation set by the United Nations.

We do not only see the United Nations as a world-wide forum; we also set great store by the possibilities provided by the United Nations of practical cooperation in diverse fields of coexistence. Thus the Federal Government welcomes and supports efforts to achieve closer technological cooperation, agreements in the disarmament field and also the manifold attempts to reduce the gulf between North and South.

On the eve of the proclamation of the Second Development Decade, the Federal Government confirms its will to cooperate in this great task. Our development policy will be guided by the strategic principles of the United Nations for the Second Decade.

The Federal Republic of Germany honours this United Nations jubilee in the firm hope that the World Organization may put its declared aims into practice with renewed strength.

Willy Brandt
Chancellor of the Federal Republic of Germany

Federal Chancellor Willy Brandt receives from Aase Lionaes the citation as Nobel Peace Prize winner for 1971.

Peace Policy in Our Time

"I See My Country's Name Linked with the Will for Peace"

Speech of Thanks by Chancellor Willy Brandt at the awarding of the 1971 Nobel Prize for Peace in Oslo on December 10th, 1971.

The great honour bestowed on me by the awarding of this prize can only, I believe, be understood as an encouragement to my political endeavours, not as a final judgement upon them. I accept this honour with a sense of the common ties linking me to all those, wherever they may be, who are doing their utmost to build a Europe of peace and to make European solidarity serve the cause of world peace.

It will not be easy for me tomorrow to make my speech about a peace which can be made in Europe, while, in other parts of the world, war is being waged and danger exists of further military confrontations.

No man can accomplish alone the task spoken of today in my connection. It is, therefore, with profound thanks that I accept the 1971 Nobel Prize for Peace on behalf also of those who are helping and have helped me.

I also feel that at this hour we are conscious of our close links with those who, acting on their beliefs, make sacrifices and still continue the struggle for peace and justice.

You will, I trust, understand when I say how glad I was in these past days and weeks to know that many — and not only in my country — believe this to be a matter which concerns them all; and, if I may say further, how much it means to me that it is my work "on behalf of the German people" which has been acknowledged; that it was granted me, after the unforgettable horrors of the past, to see the name of my country brought together with the will for peace.

In the past few weeks I have received many letters from every part of the world: from heads of state and school-children, from happy and tormented people, from a relative of Anne Frank, from prisoners. Among the first letters was one from a lady whose life had not been easy and who reminded me of the story of the Red Indian boy asking his father, as they came of the cinema: Do we never win?

Indeed, it's no wonder that many today are still asking that. I am under no illusion that I have won for them. I say only: The young man who in his time was persecuted, driven into exile in Norway and deprived of his rights as a citizen speaks here today not only in general for the cause of peace in Europe but also most particularly for those from whom the past has exacted a harsh toll.

Alfred Nobel, on the anniversary of whose death we are gathered here, said once that there is nothing in the world which cannot be misunderstood or abused. Nor should his legacy be subject to abuses or misunderstanding. But the brotherhood of peoples is a formula which grimly reminds us that Cain and Abel also were brothers: however confident our hopes, we should never forget this.

But relaxation of tensions, co-operation between peoples, reduction of forces and arms control, partnership with those who have hitherto been the losers, mutual protection against the danger of mutual destruction — this must be possible, and for this we must work.

We are here in Fridtjof Nansen's country. His help to prisoners of war, refugees and those suffering from hunger and starvation will always be a magnificent example. And in this wider sense, too, his warning holds good: make haste, lest it be too late to rue. When he came to making his will, Alfred Nobel is supposed to have said he would leave nothing to a man of action, for this would tempt him into giving up his work. He would "rather help dreamers, who find it hard to succeed in life." Well, it's not for me to judge whether the Nobel Committee has made the right choice; but this much should be known: I can hardly now afford political dreams, and I've no wish yet to give up my work.

The Nobel Prize for Peace is the highest honour, but also the most demanding, which can be granted to a man with political responsibility. I thank you sincerely and will do everything I can in my future work to bring nearer to realization what many expect of me.

"Let Me Speak of Peace Policy in Our Time...
...And About What My Own Country Can Do"

Address by Willy Brandt, Chancellor of the Federal Republic of Germany, on the occasion of the presentation of the 1971 Nobel Peace Prize in Oslo on December 11th, 1971.

The Nobel Peace Prize for 1971 has been awarded to a man still active in political life; therefore, it can only have been in appreciation of his continuing endeavours, not of his past achievements. Yesterday I expressed my gratitude; today I wish to speak about peace policy in our time: about my own experiences and, naturally, about what my own country can do, but also about what we in Europe, and from Europe, can do for the world. It is little enough, as our powerlessness in the face of the new war between India and Pakistan demonstrates.

This is precisely the time for me to re-emphasize my principles. War must not be a means of achieving political ends. Wars must be eliminated, not merely limited. No national interest can today be isolated from collective responsibility for peace. This fact must be recognized in all foreign relations. As a medium for achieving European and world-wide security, therefore, foreign policy must aim to reduce tensions and promote communication beyond frontiers.

The criterion on which Foreign Minister Walter Scheel and I orientate ourselves is that it is not enough to pronounce peaceloving intentions but that we must also endeavour actively to organize peace.

To wage war — to maintain peace; our use of language shows the challenge of peace when we see it as a permanent task.

How to prevent war is a question which is part of the European tradition — Europe has always had reason enough to ask it. The politican who in the daily conflict of interests tries to serve the cause of equitable peace draws his strength from the moral reserves that have been formed by generations before him. Consciously or not he is guided by them.

Our ethical and social concepts have been shaped by two thousand years of Christianity. And this means that, in spite of many aberrations under the flag of "the just war," attempts have been made over and over again to achieve peace in this world, too.

Our second source of strength is humanism and classical philosophy. Immanuel Kant postulated his idea of a constitutional confederation of states in words that pose a very distinct question to today's generations: Man, he said, will one day be faced with the choice of either uniting under a true law of nations or destroying with a few blows the civilization he has built up over thousands of years: then, necessity will compel him to do what he ought better to have done long ago of his own free reason.

A third strong source is socialism with its aspiration to social justice at home and abroad. And with its insistence that moral laws should find application not only between individual citizens but among nations and states. Peace policy is a sober task. I, too, try with the means at my command to pave the way for the prevalence of reason in my own country and in the world: that reason which demands that we seek peace because the absence of peace has come to mean extreme lack of reason.

War is no longer the ultima ratio but rather the ultima irratio. Even if this is not a generally held view I personally understand a policy for peace as a genuine Realpolitik of this epoch. Realpolitik as grossly abused in Germany over a period of twelve years proved to be an infernal chimera. Today we are in the process of finding a tolerable balance between ourselves and with the world. If the balance sheet of my political effectiveness were to say that I have helped to open up the way for a new sense of reality in Germany, then one of the greatest hopes of my life would have been fulfilled.

I say here what I say in Germany: A good German cannot be a nationalist. A good German knows that he cannot refuse a European calling. Through Europe, Germany returns to itself and to the constructive forces of its history. Our Europe, born of the experience of suffering and failure, is the imperative mission of reason.

II.

Under the threat of mankind's self-destruction, co-existence has become a question of the very existence of man. Co-existence became not one of several acceptable possibilities but the only chance of survival.

What is it that has characterized developments in Europe in the past 25 years? To begin with, an impressive phase of reconstruction, and secondly continued tension. The East-West conflict — the root causes of which were for the most part not in the West — has bound up many forces. During this period I was deeply involved in Berlin, the intersection of East-West tension. And let me add that I always regarded my task there — particularly in the very "militant" years — as one also of helping to safeguard peace. It was then, and still is, my conviction that if the West had allowed itself to be driven out of my city that would not only have spelt misfortune for the people directly concerned, not only great harm to the Federal Republic of Germany, Western Europe and the United States, but would most probably have had perilous consequences for peace. That was the case during Stalin's blockade of 1948, as it was when Khrushchev issued his ultimatum in 1958.

I am not one of those people who maintain or even feel that they were always right. My journey through life has always required me to ponder my own position. But I can say that ever since my youth I have been guided by those fundamental convictions that are held to lead to good neighbourliness — both at home and in relations with others.

As Mayor of Berlin I experienced how critical situations influence our thinking. I knew, though, that steadfastness serves the cause of peace.

A great deal has been written about the critical years of 1961 and 1962. Perhaps I may be allowed to add a few more comments on this period. The most striking aspect of the Berlin Wall was the absurd division of what had remained intact of the whole organism of a metropolis, with all the lamentable consequences for the people.

There were also the international implications of this incision. The Western Powers unwaveringly stood by their aegis for West Berlin. But, willy-nilly, they accepted the fact that thereby their counterpart held sole control over East Berlin. No Four-Power status did anything to alter the fact that the Wall had become the dividing line between the nuclear superpowers. And no one in a position of responsibility demanded that the Western Powers should use military force and risk a war to preserve their share of what originally was common responsibility.

There is still another aspect — that of impotence disguised by verbalism: taking a stand on legal positions which cannot become a reality and planning counter-measures for contingencies that always differ from the one at hand. At critical times we were left to our own devices; the verbalists had nothing to offer. Passionate protests were justified and necessary, but they did not alter the situation. The wall remained; we had to learn to live with it, and I had to call in the police to prevent young demonstrators from running to their ruin. The impediments on the access routes to Berlin remained. The gulf which divided Germany from Lübeck to the Czechoslovakian border also remained and grew deeper. The game with trumps that are none, as Golo Mann put it, did not change anything. It was necessary to contemplate the political possibilities anew if the people were to be aided and peace made safer.

The Cuba crisis, on a more dramatic scale and with even more at stake, showed the delimitation and the changing relations between the nuclear giants.

At the beginning of October 1962, I visited John F. Kennedy. He spoke of the danger that would emanate from missile bases aimed at the United States. I was under the impression that in Germany the danger of miscalculation could not be ruled out. There were concentrations of troops around Berlin. When, on the evening of October 23rd, President Kennedy delivered his grave speech on Cuba, he twice mentioned the connection with Berlin. I supported his view.

As it turned out, everything in our part of the world remained peaceful. The Cuba crisis was overcome by a sense of responsibility and cool-headedness. This was a significant experience and a turning-point.

A few weeks previously I had spoken at Harvard about co-existence. Judging by my experience in Berlin, I said that realistic self-confidence need not fear contact with the political and ideological antagonist; that the uncertainty of the present time must not be permitted to make us uncertain, too. What was the point, I asked, of getting into touch with the other side without being prepared to speak? Speaking surely also meant negotiating and being open to conciliation, not unilateral concessions. An active peace policy will remain for a long time to come the test of our intellectual and material vitality.

III.

After staring into the abyss of a global war we found ourselves beset by problems of global dimensions: hunger, the population explosion, environmental hazards, and the dwindling of natural resources. Only those who accept or even look forward with pleasure to the end of the world can ignore problems of such magnitude.

In our epoch the learned provide us with works that are outstanding for their expertise and deep sincerity. They are no longer merely concerned with the differences between ideologies and social systems, their concern now is the future of man and whether he has any future at all. They are concerned with problems which extend beyond the borders of individual states and beyond continents. They make a science of politics, and this science is one in which the rich, the more advanced powers must jointly participate. It is one which no country can any longer pursue for itself.

We need peace not only in the sense of the absence of violence;

we need it as the basis for that redeeming co-operation I have spoken about. And in the same way that it presupposes peace, it can help to create peace, for where there is redeeming co-operation there is peace; and there also mutual confidence will gradually establish itself. My country is no longer a "great" power, nor can it be. But it is definitely an economic and scientific power, and I feel I can say that we are all prepared for such co-operation, at any time and at any palce, however much Government and Opposition may otherwise be in dispute over this question.

I have mentioned a few aspects of what today is called peace research. It is true that a new quality in international politics has been descernible for over ten years now. The Cold War with its sterile paradox of freezing frontiers without eliminating the risk of conflict did not point the way to a solution. So the powers concerned began to keep extreme risks within bounds and to reduce tensions. In Cuba and Berlin they learned how to keep conflicts under control. De Gaulle and Nixon set the course for co-operation rather than confrontation, and Brezhnev and Kossygin began in their own way to steer towards a new relationship with the West.

On a small scale, my approach eight years ago as the Governing Mayor of Berlin was that small steps are better than no steps at all. When hundreds of thousands of people were given passes to visit their relatives over Christmas, this, in a nutshell, was the application of the knowledge that there could be a new, only apparent, paradox — and that is improving the situation by recognizing it for what it is.

Since those days and the occasion in Harvard when I developed my concept of co-existence as a challenge, taking in my term as Foreign Minister, the statement of Government policy which I made over two years ago, and the treaties of Moscow, Warsaw and Berlin, you will meet with no surprises along the course I have taken. There have been no illusions, no see-sawing. But I try to do what I said I would.

An active policy of co-existence should be based neither on fear nor on blind confidence. I know that the Western alliance would function; the potential adversary will have no illusions about this. But we must also discard that unimaginative principle that nations with different social and economic systems cannot live side by side without being in grave conflict.

Once we have got this business of living together organized with the use of force excluded and all living in safety, then we shall have to start work on the organization of co-operation. However, this aim would be doomed from the outset if its ulterior motive were a new kind of crusade. There is and will continue to be the delimitation through ideological differences. But it means progress if we speak more of interests than of ideology. It is encouraging when dialogue takes the place of monologue in East-West relations in the search for solutions to those problems which in spite of continuing differences affect common interest. The solution of mutual problems implies establishing links through meaningful co-operation among states beyond inter-bloc frontiers. This means transforming the conflict; it means doing away with actual or supposed barriers with peaceful risks on both sides. It means bulding up confidence through practical arrangements. And this confidence may then become the new basis for the solution of long-standing problems. This opportunity can be Europe's opportunity in a world which, as has been proved, cannot be ruled by Washington or Moscow — or by Peking — alone.

However unmistakably great the strength of the super-powers may be, it is an indisputable fact that other magnetic fields are emerging at the same time. Is there any point at all in drawing up a balance sheet of the future, saying that at such and such a time there will be I don't know how many super-powers? We are living in a world of the many and of change. Small nations, too, have a part in the big game; they, too, can represent power in their own way; they can be a help to themselves and to others; and they can also be a danger to themselves and to others.

The entry of the People's Republic of China into the organized system of states is not in my opinion synonymous with a transition to tripolarity; there are more than two or three centres of world power. But apart from other things there is a certain significance in the fact that the huge China is both a developing country and a nuclear power, and that in view of the ever-mounting problems in the Third World there is growing disappointment with the industrialized countries. Europe, which after the last war proved that its vitality was unbroken, still has its future ahead of itself. In the West it will grow beyond the Economic Community and — in the way that Jean Monnet sees it — develop into a union which will be able to assume part of the responsibility for world affairs, independently of the United States, but — I am sure — firmly linked with it. At the same time there are opportunities for developing co-operation and safeguarding peace throughout the whole of Europe, perhaps of establishing a kind of European Partnership for Peace; and if I were not aware of the practical and theoretical obstacles that still have to be overcome, I would even speak of a European Union of Peace.

IV.

I realize that in the annals of Nobel Prize history the Germans have been more outstanding for their achievements in the fields of chemistry and physics than for their contribution to peace. Yet in this field, too, we have our representatives. War has always called for peace, and in my country also there has at times been no want of courageous theoreticians of peace.

Take Professor Ludwig Quidde, for instance, who won the Nobel Peace Prize in 1927. The knowledge and discernment which he acquired from his historical studies inspired him to support the international anti-war movement, and for many years he was chairman of the German Peace Society. During the First World War he was an active member of the Bund Neues Vaterland (Federation for the New Fatherland) — a nice camouflage for Europe — which could boast of Ernst Reuter, the future Mayor of Berlin, as its secretary-general, and of Albert Einstein as one of its first members. Quidde, who was a member of the Bavarian legislature as early as 1907 and of the Weimar National Assembly in 1919—20, supported the principle of arbitration and was a champion of the League of Nations. Undergoing personal sacrifice, he showed democratic civil courage. He died in exile.

There is a clearer connection between me and the first German winner of the Nobel Peace Prize, Gustav Stresemann. He, too, was still active in politics when he was awarded the prize. True, we differed in some ways, not only owing to the circumstances but also as regards our personal and political temperament, and no worthy reflection on the past should attempt to even them out. And yet, rarely are achievements possible without a model from the past, and we should be able to express our gratitude for this. The First World War, like the Second, was followed by suspicions and oppressions. The era of mistrust brought the nations of Europe no further. It was Stresemann who, five years after the cease-fire, upheld the view and fought until it was accepted at home and abroad that clinging to positions long since eroded was bound to remain sterile. He was of the opinion that it was first necessary to restore the basis of trust before there could be a turn for the better. Not everybody felt as he did. There were many who thought that the mantle of mistrust should not be discarded until a number of improvements had been made. That was a problem then as it is today. The then Reich Foreign Minister was not blindly confident, but he fought — and for that he, too, needed civil courage — for a policy of conciliation, for his peace policy. It was Franco-German relations which then had suffered most under the burden of war. Nowhere else was the mountain of mistrust higher. Stresemann set about removing this, and his appeals were echoed from the other side by the man with whom he was to share the Peace Prize, Aristide Briand. What they achieved together, with the help of Britain, in Locarno was expressed by Stresemann in the following words after being presented with the Prize: "For one thing," he said, "it is the state of lasting peace on the Rhine guaranteed by a solemn untertaking by the two great neighbouring nations not to use force, guaranteed by the undertaking by other states to come to the assistance of the one who falls victim to force contrary to his solemn agreement."

You will see that what makes this sentence so important to me is the concept of renunciation of force. Malicious propaganda had at that time misunderstood or misinterpreted German policy as meaning that the Germans had renounced something which was rightfully theirs. But the truth was that we had renounced the use of force so as to give others a feeling of security and open a chapter of mutual trust.

That state of lasting peace which Stresemann spoke about was then, as we all know, again disrupted by those who, inwardly, had not renounced force. And yet I feel that what was achieved in Locarno was not to no avail. It had traced the paths which others were able to follow after yet another war.

I recall Robert Schuman, a man of so many noble ideas, on the French side, and Charles de Gaulle, the statesman who often proved to have a prophetic vision; and on the German side that conservative and constructive politican Konrad Adenauer. Not only was it given to him at an advanced age to see his life-long dream come true and Germany and France reconciled; he also played his part in making the Federal Republic an equal member of the emerging union of Western Europe and of the Atlantic alliance. Whatever our judgement of the details of these developments may have been at the time, it must be said that without the foundation that was built in the West we would not have been in a position to pursue today's aims in the East.

It was here, in the relations between Germany and her Eastern neighbours, that the greatest burdens were to be found, the highest mountain of mistrust. Here lay the task of our days. We have not by a long chalk accomplished it; in fact we have only just made a beginning, but we have taken the step in that direction and this we could only do along the paths that others had trodden before us.

European peace policy lives from the spirit of history. This does not exclude the darkest years but explicitly includes them. The award of the Nobel Peace Prize to Carl von Ossietzky during that evil era of the Hitler regime meant a great deal. Like Ludwig Quidde he had played an active part in the work of the German Peace Society. In his writings he was strongly critical of militarism and nationalism. In 1921, he wrote: "Many nations have fought against each other, but the blood that has flowed is of only one kind: the blood of Europe's citizens." That era demanded more from him than civil courage, it demanded his life.

Shortly before the presentation was made, one of those in power tried to exact from this embarrassing prisoner an assurance that he would refuse the Prize. In return he was to be set free, given financial security, and not to be bothered again in the future. Ossietzky refused and went back to prison. At that time I was 22 years old and "illegally" in Berlin, and as I had been directly involved in the "campaign" I was deeply moved by his decision.

In Carl von Ossietzky the Nobel Committee had honoured a man who had been persecuted and who could not come here to receive the Prize. That award was a moral victory over the ruling powers of barbarism. Today, in the name of free Germany, I wish to express belated thanks to the Nobel Committee for making that choice. At the same time I wish to express my appreciation and encouragement to those who help people imprisoned or persecuted in other ways on account of their conviction.

Here in particular I owe a word of deep respect to those men and women who joined the resistance against Hitler. I greet former members of the resistance movement in all countries. The German resistance fought and made sacrifices for decency, lawfulness and freedom. It preserved that Germany which I regard as my own and which has again fully become my country after the re-establishment of law and freedom.

What yesterday meant to me was that it demonstrated to the whole world that Germany has come to terms with itself, just like the German in exile was able to rediscover the peaceful and human features of his fatherland.

V.

When I was still Foreign Minister I said that the policy of our country must unequivocally be orientated to the safeguarding of peace as its common denominator. The present Foreign Minister and I know, of course, that peace policy must be something more than merely applauding others. Everyone must ask himself what specific contribution he should make. Particularly a country like the Federal Republic of Germany could not remain tied to a vaguely general, but had to define a specific contribution. We could not leave to others answers which we could give ourselves.

Nobody can relieve us of a task when, owing to the realities of the situation, it is one that only we ourselves can fulfil.

I said the realities of the situation. These we cannot recognize if we are prone to self-deception or if we confuse politics with legal arguments. The Kremlin is no local court, said President Paasikivi, and I would extend this metaphor to include Washington. I knew that the bill for Hitler's war was still unpaid, but I have never been of a mind to negotiate on the principles of human rights and self-determination.

Looking at the matters from the realities of the situation, that meant not questioning any one's territorial integrity but rather recognizing the inviolability of frontiers. When we proposed a treaty on the renunciation of force and called upon our Eastern neighbours to take us at our word we were able to build on what other federal governments before us had said and to which they had pledged themselves in the treaties with the Western countries. The logical consequence of our policy was that the inviolability of frontiers also had to apply to our relations with Eastern Europe and to relations between the two states in Germany which had become members of the two alliance systems.

The tension — between the will for peace and self-assertion — which governed the work of the German politician during the period of confrontation led via passionate disputes to the clarification of major problems. The result has been our East-West policy. We have taken the dictate of self-assertion seriously, and we have not let the idea of national unity fall into decay. On the contrary, we have set about reorganizing our relationship with Eastern Europe in our own national interest as well. This is not simply a succession of measures and treaties, but an extensive and manifold process designed to use all possible ways of reducing the relative importance of frontiers and of opening up new paths.

I do not like the label Ostpolitik, but how can one take back something that has almost become a by-word and, like Gemütlichkeit almost untranslatable, accepted international terminology? The word is tinged with connotations of the past. And it could lead to misinterpreting foreign policy as if it were a chest of drawers which can be opened at random. In actual fact our policy of détente began in the West and remains rooted in the West. We want and need both partnership with the West and conciliation with the East.

No one should overlook the fact that Western European unification, in which we are playing an active part, remains our priority aim. The Atlantic alliance is indispensable to us. Yet, not only the development of the world situation in general, but also the special reality of the treaties with the West require them to be supplemented by normal and, where possible, friendly relations with the Soviet Union and its partners in the Warsaw Pact. In this I am in agreement with President Pompidou, with Prime Ministers Heath and Colombo, in fact with all our friends and allies.

Because it will benefit ourselves, the Germany in the two states of the one nation, we shall ratify our treaties with the Soviet Union and the People's Republic of Poland. One of the Federal Government's aims is to establish a relaxed and fruitful relationship with the other members of the Warsaw Pact also. Our relations with the GDR will, in spite of all the difficulties, and respecting the rights and responsibilities of the Four Powers for Germany as a whole, be organized on the bases of equality in the form customary in international relations. The negotiations between the two parts of Germany with a view to filling in the framework provided by the Quadripartite Agreement on Berlin have shown that complicated matters can be settled even where legal views are irreconcilable.

The Federal Republic knows the limits of its possibilities. At the same time it is conscious that it definitely possesses power and is a power — it regards itself as a power fully in the service of peace. The transition from classical power politics to the business-like peace policy we are pursuing must be understood as the change of objective and method from the imposition to the balancing of interests. This calls for self-conquest, an objective approach and an appraisal of our political strength and possibilities that is in no way less realistic than the classical concept of power politics would demand. This appraisal should lead from sacred national egoism to a European and global domestic policy which feels responsible for ensuring that man everywhere has an existence worthy of human dignity.

VI.

Turning now to a few of the elements that could go to make up a European peace pact, I will not tarry to consider institutional concepts which cannot in any case be put into effect in the short term. But I re-emphasize my faith in the universal principles of general international law, however, much they may be disregarded. They found binding expression in the principles of the United Nations Charter: sovereignty — territorial integrity — non-violence — the right of self-determination of nations — human rights.

These principles are inalienable even though their application is often imperfect — that I know. Incidentally, one of the hardships in the life of the politician, especially the head of the Government, is that he cannot always say what he thinks, that for the sake of peace he cannot always give vent to his feelings. Moreover, I am convinced that all-European security and co-operation will not be impaired by the continued progress of West European unification. Western Europe including Britain, the enlarging Community therefore, is not forming itself into a bloc against Eastern Europe, but it can, by strengthening its social components also, develop into an especially important element in the building of a balanced European system of security. Firmly rooted cohesion internally need not be inconsistent with an outward-looking co-operative approach.

I would also say that Europe and America cannot be separated. They need each other as self-confident, equal partners. The heavier the burden the United States has to carry, the more will that great country be able to rely on our friendship.

The points I am outlining are realistically based on the assumption that we must first of all take the world with its systems and ideologies as it stands today. Knowing full well the degree of imperfection we encounter, we must nonetheless attempt to build a structure of peace which will be more durable than former systems and egoisms, and which can be further improved. First, this means that our all-European policy cannot ignore the centuries-old identities of nations and states. In fact, we shall have to establish a balance between states und groups of states in which each will preserve its identity and security. But such a balance must be something more than just a balance of military power.

Second, once and for all and without exception we must renounce force and the threat of force in relations between states. This includes of necessity the inviolability of existing frontiers. But the integrity of frontiers cannot mean cementing them as barriers between enemies.

Third, beyond a general renunciation of force — whether bilateral or multilateral — we can achieve more security through the equal participation of the nations of Europe in specific agreements on arms limitation and control. There will have to be concrete negotiations on balanced force reductions in Central Europe.

Fourth, the principle of non-interference in the internal affairs of other states must be respected, but non-interference is not enough. A Europe living in peace calls for its members to be willing to listen to the arguments of others, for the struggle of convictions and interests will continue. Europe needs tolerance. It needs freedom of thought, not moral indifference.

Deeply moved, Chancellor Brandt accepted in the company of his wife the congratulations from Chancellory officials on the occasion of his being awarded the Nobel Peace Prize.

Numerous citizens of Bonn, the capital of West Germany, honoured the 1971 Nobel Peace Prize winner with a torch parade.

Shortly after it became known that Chancellor Willy Brandt had been awarded the Nobel Peace Prize for 1971, he was congratulated by the Chairmen of the three political parties presently represented in the Bundestag. Above, Herbert Wehner of the SPD and Wolfgang Mischnick of the FDP. Below, Chairman of the CDU/CSU opposition, Doctor Barzel.

Fifth, the time is ripe for the development of new forms of economic, technological and scientific co-operation and for the building up of an all-European infrastructure. And above all: Europe evolved as a cultural community, and it should again become what it was.

Sixth, social security is one of the foundations of lasting peace. Material want is in effect bondage and, in Europe at any rate, it must be overcome by evolution.

Seventh, Europe must live up to its world-wide responsibility. This means co-responsibility for world peace, and it must also mean co-responsibility for justice towards the outside world so that hunger and misery elsewhere can be overcome. Peace is something more than the absence of war, although some nations would be thankful for that alone today. A durable and equitable peace system requires equal development opportunities for all nations.

Our object in this respect is not to pursue far-off abstract targets but to deal with differences as soberly as possible. I know that to some, especially among the young generation, this is too little and that to many people the whole process is too slow anyway. It is not harmful but rather helpful when young people revolt against the disproportion between outdated structures and new possibilities, and when they protest against the contradiction of semblance and reality. I do not believe in saying what young people expect me to say, but I appeal to them to use their unspent energies in critical and responsible co-operation with us.

What we need is a sense of proportion, resolution and endurance. And of course we also need to have an eye for new dimensions and the energy to cope with them. In view of the magnitude of the tasks facing us, we require a healthy mixture of faith in the future and sober realism. Incidentally, can there be anything more important than helping to organize Europe and peace?

VII.

In the field of practical politics there are two tasks not far ahead: a conference on security and co-operation in Europe and negotiations on force reductions. At the same time, irrespective of whether they are members of blocs or not, the nations of Europe must begin to develop economic, technological and cultural co-operation commensurate with the size of the projects that will need to be implemented in the development of Europe. And in pursuing this objective national frontiers must be no obstacle.

The conference will have to consider the possibilities of co-operation and at the same time questions of security. I perceive the possibility of creating through economic and other ties between

East and West, North and South in Europe common interests and responsibilities which will produce more security for all. Renunciation of force must become a law which every state respects and which rules out interference. Along this road, which will certainly not be a short one, we can arrive at a system of security in Europe superimposed on the blocs, as it were; judging by the world situation, that system is feasible neither without the United States nor without the Soviet Union.

Balanced force reductions can pave the way towards that aim. I helped to formulate the "signal of Reykjavik" in the spring of 1968 and naturally I have not forgotten the setback which we all witnessed soon afterwards. The road ahead will continue to be stony. Those who have followed the history of global or regional agreements which the Geneva Disarmament Committee has achieved through painstaking efforts over the past ten years — Antarctic, test ban, space, non-proliferation, seabed, and biological weapons — feel encouraged in spite of everything. Together with others, the superpowers, in spite of all their differences, are finding partial areas of common interest in the safeguarding of peace.

And I feel even more encouraged for a special reason: This year I have put to President Nixon and Mr. Brezhnew separately the same questions on various aspects of force reductions, and received favourable answers from both of them. The leaders of the most powerful nations are also wondering whether they cannot make available more money for other than military purposes.

VIII.

There are strong forces in opposition to the organization of peace. We have witnessed the barbarism into which man can relapse. No religion, no ideology, no glorious cultural evolution can rule out for certain the possibility of hatred breaking out from the innermost depths of the human heart and plunging nations into disaster. Peace, like freedom, is no original state which existed from the start; we shall have to make it, in the truest sense of the word.

To achieve this we shall have to know more about the origin of conflicts. This is where the institutions of peace and conflict research are faced with huge tasks. As I see it, next to reasonable politics, learning is in our world the true credible alternative to force.

Another opposing force we have to contend with is the sacro egoismo of pressure groups. We still see them in Europe practically every day, and the unbridled national egoism of young states is developing so quickly that it seems to have no difficulty in catching up with the old nations who have many centuries' start. Ideologies, their harbingers and followers over and over again disregard the fundamental ethical principles of co-existence because they want to "improve" mankind, to preserve the purity of their doctrine, or to get the better of other doctrines. It is not possible to sow the seeds of lasting peace between such forces. A policy for peace must make them understand that neither states nor ideologies are ends in themselves but that they are there to serve the individual in his efforts to live and develop his life meaningfully.

The quest for absolute possession is a threat to man. Those who feel they own the entire truth, those who will have the paradise of their dreams here and now, destroy only too easily the ground on which a system allowing for human dignity can grow. The tradition of European democracy, too, knows not only of a humanitarian but also of a doctrinaire trait which leads to tyranny; liberation then becomes slavery.

Young people often expect me to give an unqualified "Yes," a clear "No." But it has become impossible for me to believe in one, in the single truth, so I say to my young friends and to others who want to hear it: There are several truths, not merely the one truth which excludes all others. That is why I believe in diversity and hence in doubt. It is productive. It questions existing things. It can be strong enough to smash fossilized injustice. Doubt proved its worth during the resistance. It is tough enough to outlast defeats and to disillusion victors.

Today we know how rich and at the same time how limited man is in his possibilities. We know him in his aggression and in his brotherliness. We know that he is capable of applying his inventions for his own good, but also of using them to destroy himself. Let us drop all these terrible excessive demands. I believe in active compassion and therefore in man's responsibility. And I believe in the absolute necessity of peace.

As a democratic socialist my thoughts and my work are orientated to change. Not that I want to remodel man, for to force him into a system means to destroy him, but I believe in the changeability of human conditions.

During my life I have seen many illusions develop and disappear; much confusion, escapism and simplification. In one place a sense of responsibility was lacking, in another imagination. I have also experienced what faith in one's convictions, steadfastness and solidarity can mean. I know how moral strength can develop and emerge especially in times of great affliction. Many things declared dead have proved to be alive.

Originally Alfred Nobel thought that he would have his Peace Prize awarded only six times once every five years, after which it would no longer be necessary. It has in fact lasted longer, otherwise I would not have had the opportunity of addressing you here today.

Bertha von Suttner, who was awarded the Prize in 1905, overestimated the favourable response to her book "Lay Down Your Arms." I am still one of those who were deeply impressed by the book, and after all else I gladly identify myself with the naive Humanism of my youth.

But I cannot end my speech without reminding you and myself of those who at this moment are living and suffering in war, especially on the Indian subcontinent and in Vietnam. I include also the people living in the Middle East and other areas of crises. I do not feel like making loud appeals, for it is easy to demand moderation, reason and modesty of others. But this plea comes from the bottom of my heart: May all those who possess the power to wage war have the mastery of reason to maintain peace.

"My Countrymen Want to Be Good Neighbours Both Among Themselves and Towards Others"

Speech of Chancellor Willy Brandt at the Storkyrkan in Stockholm on December 12th, 1971.

Let me thank you for the great kindness you have shown me and for what Alva Myrdal has said.

So many marks of appreciation have poured in on me in the past days and weeks but I am only conditionally entitled to them. I alone cannot accept nor do them justice. And this is also true for the expectations. I share the burden with many who are working for peace; with all those who strive for it sincerely, in whatever country, whatever position, whatever party they may be. To you, my friends in Sweden, I give my sincere good wishes. And I am glad that here as elsewhere many feel personally affected and encouraged by what is given expression in the Nobel Prize for Peace.

Let us think of the people who today must live in the midst of war. Let us especially affirm our common ties with those who are persecuted because they strive for peace and human rights.

I should like here to thank all those who — in Sweden or whatever country — are involved in humanitarian work. Service on behalf of one's fellow-men is work for the cause of peace.

And let us say to those working in the field of development aid that they should never grow weary, for their work, which must be intensified and expanded, is in the service of peace.

It is not for me to make any judgement on my own endeavours. I am still in pursuit of the goal, not at the end; indeed, I believe, there never will be an end.

In the struggle for peace — and that means today, for the survival of mankind — each individual must ask himself what he himself can do. What he can persuade his own country to do; what its specific contribution should be.

My country's task was to put behind it the sombre past without forgetting it.

It had the task of complementing our friendship with the West by reconciliation with the East.

It has the ambition, after bitter experiences, to demonstrate that its people are good neighbours, both among themselves and towards others.

To achieve a European peace treaty — and in the course of developments perhaps even a European alliance for peace — that is a task which even a few years ago seemed impossible to accomplish. I believe that we can now come closer to achieving this. If we allow ourselves no illusions; if we proceed on the basis of our common interests, rather than divisive ideologies.

Nobody should misjudge the seriousness of the situation: Peace, even in our part of the world, is still far from being secured. Hard effort is still needed.

Finally a very personal word: I am indebted to Sweden not only because for five years I found refuge here; not only because I learned much here; not only because, as Mayor of Berlin, I have experienced what is meant by Swedish altruism; but also because on the way towards an understanding between West and East I received most valuable support from this country.

Again I thank you all sincerely. And I ask, just as sincerely, that we may never weary in the struggle to secure peace in Europe; and all that a peaceful Europe can give to the world.

Peace Efforts Are "Hard Work on Stony Ground"

Speech delivered by the Chancellor of the Federal Republic of Germany, Willy Brandt, in the Storkyrkan, Stockholm, on December 12th, 1971.

I.

I am grateful for the invitation to speak to you here in this beautiful old church. For the strong and friendly interest shown in the Nobel Peace Prize. And last, but not least, for the understanding and encouraging words of welcome with which Provost Kastlund has addressed me.

No one finds it easy to speak about peace in Europe while people in other parts of the world have to live in a state of war. That is why, from this rostrum, too, I would ask that all those who have the power to wage war may command the reason which is necessary to preserve or restore peace. The great honour bestowed upon me by the award of this Peace Prize should not, I feel, be taken as relating to me alone. So I stand here as one of many who during these years, in many countries and at different levels of responsibility, have been devoting their efforts to organizing peace in Europe, and while doing so, are not losing sight of what the world expects of Europe.

Everybody must know that this is hard work on stony ground, and that it is not only praise nor even approbation one earns for it. But praise and approbation are less important than tenacious pursuance of what one has discerned to be right.

Everybody must know, too, that today he is required to do more than accompany others with applause or critical marginal notes. Every individual bearing responsibility and feeling responsible must ask himself: What can I do to help? And what is the special contribution my country can make? And thus it has been my duty to answer this question with regard to my country.

It has been anything but a matter of course that this Peace Prize has been awarded to a German. Many of my countrymen have been deeply moved by this. I have drawn encouragement from letters such as the one from a survivor of a concentration camp or the letter of a man convicted in connection with the war who has now been serving his sentence for more than 26 years. Women and men of the most varied groups of my people have written to me that now they felt the spell of mistrust had been broken, and perhaps they no longer feel so ashamed of the disgrace that had come upon our nation; they could now feel proud of Germany again.

Such comments should not be misunderstood. No nation, however deep it may have fallen, can and wants to live without pride forever. The boundless cruelty of the Hitler regime seemed to have made the European judgement of the Germans irreversible. It has not been easy to keep alive faith in a decent Germany.

However, it is not only the individual who can think things over and mend his ways. A nation, too, can overcome an evil past and re-define its place in history.

Like me, many of my countrymen would have breathed a sigh of relief if the gallant men of our internal resistance on July 20th, 1944, had succeeded at least at that late stage in setting a premature end to that destructive madness. Instead, we in Germany, and in Europe, had to struggle and suffer our way through the bitter aftermath of the war and the Cold War, utnil a new Germany was able to participate actively in organizing peace — a Germany that has found its image in the Federal Republic as a state based on a liberal system obeying the rule of law.

Chancellor Adenauer was able to accomplish the first important part, namely, to build up understanding and trustful co-operation with the countries of the West. Ours was the task of tackling the equally important second part; that is, reconciliation with our neighbours in the East and all-European co-operation leading beyond and overriding the East-West conflict.

Yesterday, in Oslo, I spoke about what, from my point of view and experience, European peace policy should be in our day and age. And that we should neither undertake too much nor too little. That we need absolute renunciation of force; a reduction and, if possible, also contorl of armaments. And in spite of all continuing differences and conflicts a network of practical co-operation spanning all Europe: economic, technical and scientific, as well as cultural. And also more tolerance, more readiness to hear and weigh up the other party's arguments.

II.

It cannot be our intention to remould the nature of man. What is essential, however, is to change his living conditions and some of his behaviour. It is the only possible way of achieving peace and good-neighbourly relations within and without.

As you know, I am a democratic socialist, and as such I draw from the sources of Christian ethics, of humanism and of classical philosophy. We who live in an area bearing the hall-marks of Christianity do not only seek peace in eternity but certainly also peace in man's time. It is the theme of the New Testament which thus responds to man's longing. Peace on earth is a promise; we do not need to wait for it but have to work for it by deeds. It will not be fulfilled without any doing of our own.

Who would know this better than Protestantism, which has inspired the Scandinavian men of faith in their work for peace? I would, at this point, recall Archbishop Söderblom, whose memory lives forth. He was one of the great men of our century — great in his faith, in his thinking, in his work. He not only gave powerful impulses to the ecumenical movement between the two wars, but had even before that, during World War I, impressed upon the church its obligation to work for peace.

Looking beyond Christian fraternity he had said: Christians must always try to understand what is at the root of other people's thoughts and actions. And they must work with all their might for understanding between nations. When Nathan Söderblom accepted the Nobel Peace Prize in Oslo in December 1930 he spoke of the broad way and the straight way. On the broad way, he said, where man leaves his complacency and his inferior qualities at rest, peace is beyond reach. Only the straight way, on which man does not leave himself at rest, leads to peace. For him there was the straight way only the way "which means conversion." He also emphasized at the time that the search for peace must become more realistic if it was to be of any consequence at all. The question is not, he said, whether you are orthodox by one peace formula or another, but whether you really do something for peace. My sincere thanks go to all those who really have done something.

By this I mean not least the humanitarian aid granted to so many refugees and other distressed people while the war lasted and to an increased extent, after it had ended. I know from my Berlin days what Swedish soup meant for the children. I mention no names nor organizations — I mean all and everybody who participated in the noble work of helping the afflicted and the persecuted. And all those who helped to make help possible.

One might say that this has nothing to do with the prevention of war but only with the mitigation of its consequences. I feel, however, that relief work is work for peace because it saves lives, it represses despair and resuscitates hope. This also holds for non-official development aid in particular, for the struggle against hunger and distress in the Third World. My own life has taught me what distress is like. I know, too, what it means to bei persecuted and outlawed. Sweden and the North have opened their hearts and made survival possible for many thousands. The tradition personified by Fridtjof Nansen and Folke Bernadotte has remained alive. And for that I owe additional thanks.

What I have particularly at heart is to express my appreciation and encouragement to all those who, in this country and others, so untiringly and unselfishly espouse the cause of imprisoned and persecuted people. Who seek to ensure that they are treated in keeping with the standards of human dignity and, where possible, are amnestied. And that the principle of the rule of law is increasingly applied in all parts of the world.

The struggle for peace and the struggle for human rights are inseparable.

III.

My indebtedness to this country extends in particular to the ideal values it imparts. I recall that we — when here as refugees — were not doomed to intellectual frustration, but could learn and develop. That there were people we could talk to and who took us seriously.

I will name here Alva and Gunnar Myrdal, as two among many. These two remarkable and unusually productive people were never short of work, not during the war either. But they took their time to deliberate with us on postwar tasks. We, that was a group of stragglers from the occupied and destroyed countries. And our central subjects were the objectives of peace, the dictates of reason as against the aberrations of hatred. In politics, no one can work forward who is without hope. When Alva und Gunnar Myrdal received a German peace prize in Frankfurt last year, they were praised for their unshakeable faith in man's reason. Which results in the hope that an unillusioned and purposeful effort may ultimately still lead to success. Their fields of activity extend beyond their own country and Europe, but have much to do with that for which Europe's energies must be mobilized.

The struggle for disarmament is toilsome and has so far been altogether depressing. And yet there is a growing realization that we cannot be content with the balance of nuclear terror.

The fact is that the negotiations between the two superpowers about the limitation of strategic arms show initial concrete results. With its proposal for the banning of biological weapons, the Geneva Committee of the United Nations General Assembly has, for the first time, been able to submit a genuine disarmament agreement, which is more than a limitation agreement. And at the same time we are approaching the point from where the mutual balanced reduction of force levels and armaments in Europe can presumably be discussed.

All this will be most difficult and take more time than we would like. But there is a growing realization of the new requirements and possibilities.

The essential point is that world peace must be understood to be a vital living condition of the technical age, and that we must find global answers to problems affecting the globe as a whole. It would be absurd to view aid for the Third World and protection from environmental dangers as two competing tasks instead of treating them as two dimensions of world domestic policy.

The industrial world has begun to grow conscious of the enclaves of poverty and backwardness existing in its midst. But it must not forget the distress in the Southern hemisphere. What we see there is more than courage born of despair. I would not have thought it possible, for instance, that large countries would be able over a span of a few years to raise their agricultural production so as to meet their own requirements.

At the same time, the present war on the Indian subcontinent demonstrates the close proximity of hope and disillusionment. We should, in any case, not allow ourselves to be misled by too optimistic a construction. Millions of people die year after year of the direct and indirect consequences of hunger. And it seems that nothing can change the fact that humanity will have doubled to between six and seven thousand million people by the turn of the century, that is, in thirty years.

The experts say, and I believe they are right: The circle of misery can only be broken at its crucial point if we succeed in the seventies — in the Second Development Decade — in improving education, employment, the food supply, housing, the health service and social security in such a way that visible successes in family planning will become possible in the eighties. It is by no means a matter of helping a natural development process on. What is necessary is to replace a destroyed social balance and to seek a new dynamic one. Each country will have to find its own way towards that goal — even if it leads through unavoidable tension. But, more than hitherto, the overall task requires planned, common and internationally concerted action.

And then: When the natural resources of water, oxygen and living substances on this planet come to an end, there will be left a poisoned and starving human race which will no longer be asking for an organized peace such as we are striving for today. The question is how the finite resources of this earth will have to be administered — which is indispensable in order to preserve man's biological existence. This question will be raised in more and more concrete terms and will have to be answered.

Their common interest in survival should not force the states with different ideologies and social systems to waste their energies but join them for the solution of objectively common problems. No one can escape this realization who is not indifferent to this world's coming to an end.

Here in Stockholm the large United Nations Conference on Environment Problems will convene next year. I do hope it will show itself equal to the significance of the task.

And there is another thing I would say to the address of political and industrial leaders in the developed states: We should all make our constructive contribution towards ensuring that the next United Nations Trade and Development Conference, taking place in Santiago, will not turn out a bitter disappointment to the developing countries and hence a failure, but will re-open the way ahead.

IV.

For us in Europe it is essential to take more and more substance out of the East-West conflict which has already been mitigated, and to overcome it as far as possible. To do that we must start from the real facts — whether we like them or not — such as they have evolved as a consequence of World War II. It means that we must start from the inviolability of frontiers.

To recognize existing frontiers cannot mean the intention to cement them. To renounce force does not mean to renounce the struggle for humanitarian improvements and the application of human rights. However, some realities can only be changed for the better after one has taken note of them.

In Europe it is essential to arrive at more communication and co-operation beyond the boundaries of blocs and ideologies. This I am trying to achieve with the possibilities my country offers and which certainly are limited, and naturally in unison with our allies. I know that much depends on this for a lasting peace in Europe. It is only that we must not and will not wait with preparations for a European pact of peace until the laborious process of achieving a normal situation and understanding has been concluded. These two processes are interdependent with and complementary to each other.

One can prepare a European pact of peace by agreements on the renunciation of force. One can combine elements of security with those of co-operation. And one can convene conferences in order to consider new tasks. All this will keep as long and as far as the cover of mutual confidence reaches and depends on the strength of the will for peace.

On the other hand, that will needs to be expressed in terms of treaties. Thus, there are some treaties we have concluded with our Eastern neighbours and others we have prepared. And so we have furthered the Berlin Agreement of the Four Powers and conducted the supplementary intra-German negotiations. Against this background we have expressed our readiness to help prepare a conference on security and co-operation in Europe provided that the United States and Canada participate. And at the same time we are ready, like others, to co-operate constructively in negotiations on a reduction of forces in Europe.

In other words, I maintain that peace can be organized, that it can be made. But I am aware that this requires a great effort and conscientious preparations. Peace must — as Kant long ago observed — be based on agreement. This, on the other hand, can only be achieved by the cooperation of many. Organized peace must be measurable by concrete results. For it should and must be more than the absence of war and military pressure. Peace should be understood as being something active, something with a new moral, and not only practical quality.

I am not a dreamer. I know that the elementary arguments about ideas and interests will continue. But what is essential is that this struggle of opinions and interests does not generate the causes of new wars.

The balance of terror must not set us at rest. We need additional security. What we need is conclusions drawn from the realization that world peace has become a vital living condition of our technical age.

Beyond regional groupings we need multi-faceted European co-operation. Abraham Lincoln said that a house divided against itself cannot stand. This applies to Europe as well.

The Bishop of Berlin-Brandenburg has kindly pointed out to me that the Biblical device for the day on which the Norwegian Nobel Committee awarded me the Peace Prize was: "I have caused thee to rest from thine enemies." (Samuel 2, Ch. 7, 11). Well, I suppose, none of us can venture to hope for this. But it could be progress if many of those who, like me, bear responsibility did not block the way towards fulfilling this promise.